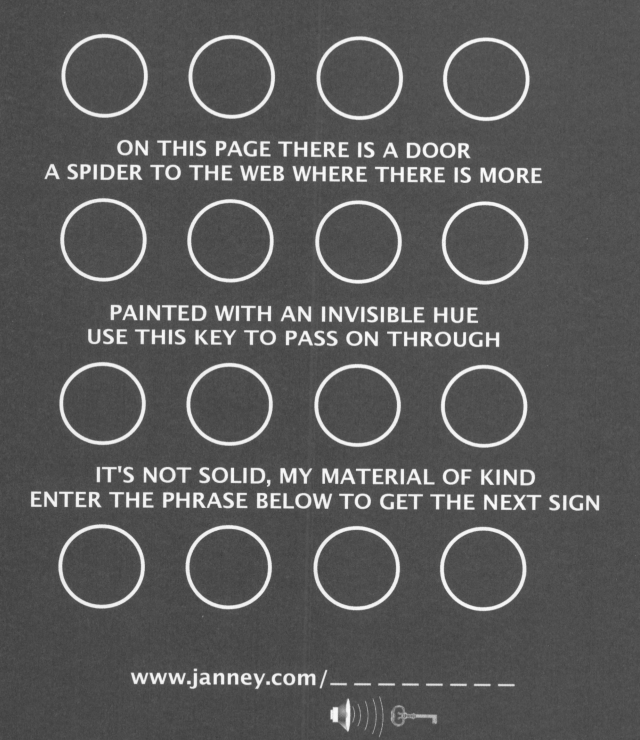

ON THIS PAGE THERE IS A DOOR
A SPIDER TO THE WEB WHERE THERE IS MORE

PAINTED WITH AN INVISIBLE HUE
USE THIS KEY TO PASS ON THROUGH

IT'S NOT SOLID, MY MATERIAL OF KIND
ENTER THE PHRASE BELOW TO GET THE NEXT SIGN

www.janney.com/_ _ _ _ _ _ _ _ _

Architecture
of the Air

To Atlantis Global —

A great company!
Hope to work together.
Best,

Charly

58/2000

. . . when sound is thrust into the sky as an inventive idea,
   is like a wondrous sleek building—an eagle soaring above it—
   architecture can create memorable language up there
   pointing fingers up toward where religion swears God is,
   where we know the spirit of great poetry sings & lives

Quincy Troupe, *The Architecture of Language,* (dedicated to Christopher Janney and others)

Architecture of the Air

The Sound and Light Environments of

Christopher Janney

Foreword by Sir George Martin
Essay by Beth Dunlop
Project Texts by Ellen Lampert-Gréaux

Produced by Sideshow Media, LLC, New York, NY

Editorial director: Dan Tucker
Cover and interior designer: Claudia Brandenburg
"Sonic Reflections" designers: Carol Bankerd, Amy Bernhardt
Photo researchers: Kathryn Williams, Rebecca Seltzer

Printed in China

Available to the trade in the United States and Canada through Baker & Taylor

ISBN: 0-9788143-0-4

Acknowledgments

This started out as a catalogue for an exhibition on my work. Where it has ended, I am not sure, but it has been quite a ride. First of all, I want to thank Beth Dunlop. It's been three years since she and I first spoke, at a Miami Heat game, about writing something on my work. Since then, we enlisted Dan Tucker of Sideshow Media to put it all together. Dan, in turn, picked Claudia Brandenburg (a good musical name) to be the book's designer and enlisted researchers Kathryn Williams and Rebecca Seltzer, who spent countless hours poring over images and details.

For my essay, "Sonic Reflections," I realized early on that I wanted it to be more than text and images; in the spirit of Ram Dass's *Be Here Now* and Lawrence Halprin's *The RSVP Cycles*, the layout had to also make a statement about my thought and creative processes. For this, I asked my former teacher and friend of thirty years, Carol Bankerd, together with computer jock Amy Bernhardt, to design this section with me.

While creating *David's Way*, a work commissioned by the Meyerson family, I let slip that we were working on a book/catalogue and exhibition. The Meyerson Foundation generously helped to underwrite the book—among other endeavors, including the first "Resonating Frequencies" series—so we could have the freedom to create the work I envisioned without compromise. To them, everyone on this project owes a deep sense of gratitude for allowing us to keep the vision intact. As well, along the way, I had support from the Graham Foundation and the New York State Council on the Arts.

I also want to thank two of my writer friends, Richard Ben Cramer (who promptly told me "it's not English") and Mike Sager, for constructive input and feedback.

Lastly, almost every acknowledgement has the author thanking some members of his family. First, to my parents "Phred" and Mary Janney—part too-overbearing, part laissez-faire (it was the sixties), I now know every parent has to improvise. Perhaps most important, they valued education and made every opportunity available to me that they could. Now it is my turn to pass this gift on to my children.

My deepest thanks go to my always friend, parental partner, and sometimes wife, Terrell Lamb. Daily lunch with her has always been a special treat. In addition, her editing and continual comments pushed this project along. ("It's nice to read. When I'm mad at you, it helps me to remember why I married you.")

And, of course, my two angels, Freddy and Lilli, now teenagers with a little devilishness creeping in. They remind me why I create this work, why I want to put work in the public realm, why I want to try to affect social change and leave the planet a more interesting place than I found it.

Staff who have worked at/with PhenomenArts, Inc., during the time of these projects include:

Joy McLaughlin	Phil Franklin	George Quaiver	Andrea DeVries
Kristin Loheed	Mike Dwyer	Brandon Dengler	Leslie Capachietti
Mike Wiggins	Pat Voyajopoulos	Richie Israel	Don Maillett
John Monticone	Jamie Coccolutto	Reid Adams	Geoff Pingree
Mark Wong	Justin Keith	Eric Wild	Gordon Stott
Bill Codington	Gabrielle Riley	Junichi Katagiri	
Tim McLaughlin	Mark Orleans	David O'Brien	

And last but not least, other friends who have been an inspiration to the work over the years:

Otto Piene	Sara Rudner	Jed Wheeler	James Seawright
Herbie Hancock	Chris Ballew	Elise Bernhardt	Bernardo Fort Brescia
Joe Zawinul	Stan Strickland	Wayne Naus	Philip Glass
Claes Oldenburg	John Ryan	John Cage	Ivan Tcherepnin
Aviva Davidson	Martha Schwartz	John Hejduk	Laurinda Spear
Bob Rauschenberg	Laurie Anderson	Jack Langstaff	Richard Pilkinton
Peter Sellars	Quincy Troupe	Sir George Martin	Jesse Sayre
Wes Wirth	Ed Grenga		

Foreword
by
Sir George Martin

Having spent an entire lifetime involved in music in one form or another, I guess it is natural for me to believe that it is the most sublime of all the arts—the most mysterious, the most primitive, the nearest to the soul. It can touch the heart in a way that nothing else can. But that does not mean that music is without design. Design is at the very heart of the universe, and man is at his finest when he uses his intelligence to design great works.

I have always thought that music is closely linked with sculpture, the art of space, and this is just a short step to the ingenuity of architecture, so that one can feel the solidity of form in music and explore its spaces as one might run one's hands over a sculpture by Henry Moore.

Nowadays, one is able to listen to a great deal of good music and to see fine buildings. However, I have to admit that I have all too often heard deadly monotonous musical works that for sheer ugliness rival some of the vast slabs of concrete blocks that may be found in the worst of our urban areas.

Conversely, in the golden age of music, when Bach wrote his glorious *St. Matthew Passion*—surely one of the greatest compositions ever conceived— he was designing a towering cathedral of sound, carving intricate designs along soaring pillars that reached out for God himself. And Bach did it all without the help of computers, synthesizers, or electronic aids.

Christopher Janney is an extraordinary man. His designs—whether they are for a university or a beach house, an airport concourse or a plain dining table—are always a revelation. He straddles the worlds of architecture and music as though they comprise a single sphere. His inventive and restless mind is continually searching for—and finding—new ideas and experiences. In our scary high-tech age, he has been able to sup with the devil and yet use, for the good, aspects of modern technology that many of us find bewildering. He is, without doubt, a twenty-first-century man, whose curiosity knows no bounds, and he can be relied upon to surprise and delight us with his work.

Christopher Janney and Sir George Martin at Abbey Road Studios, London, November 2005.

Introduction
by
Beth Dunlop

Christopher Janney defies categorization. Much of his work, done in the course of a career that has now spanned three decades, can be considered public art—large-scale commissions for such civic buildings as airports or libraries. "Urban Musical Instruments," he likes to call them, a name that is most apt. The work transforms facades, gateways, entry porticoes, entire buildings, parks, plazas, airport concourses, and even subway platforms in the way that the best of the genre can—making us stop, look, and listen. Yet for all that his work transforms public places, Janney does not think of himself as a public artist so much as an architect, by training, whose work delves into the worlds of sight and sound, or perhaps as a musician whose work probes and alters the physical realm. We are accustomed to putting almost everything, including art, into tidy categorical boxes. When the equation changes, there is no real definition for the result.

Consider this: Janney's work can only exist because of architecture and as part of architecture, but—even in the two houses he has built—it is not architecture as we traditionally think of it. Most (though not all) of the time, his efforts are collaborations with architects who have designed buildings and public boards who have commissioned them. The work relies both on musical composition—be it actual music, archival voices, or recorded sound—and illumination, and, in so doing, it merges with architecture, with the built environment, to transcend any one of these disciplines and become art of the public realm.

Janney takes all of our ordinary suppositions and turns them upside down or inside out, or both, challenging us to think about the world in an entirely different way—as a collection of animated, vibrant, living entities that connect with us to stimulate our senses. Thus, he expands our notion of architecture and art. "I think you can hear color," he once said, posing what are at best improbabilities, at least to most of us. "I think you can see sound."

Indeed, the work that Janney creates so intertwines color and sound with the more tangible world of structure that one *does* begin to hear color and see sound. So if these are improbabilities, they are also challenges. In an era when far too many public buildings are reduced to little more than functionality—victims of unimaginative architecture and "value engineering" that strips away quality and detailing—Janney is able to animate what were bland facades,

A building in Liverpool, UK.

energize barren plazas, illuminate bleak and empty passageways, and otherwise fill in the blanks.

One cannot see this work as a critique of architecture, however, but rather more as a compassionate and vividly imaginative approach to understanding and enhancing civic spaces and public places. Indeed, if it is a critique of any sort, it would be of the ways in which we as a society, as a culture, have lost our imagination, lost our connection with the environment—built or otherwise—and are cut off from a larger universe of possibilities.

I first encountered Christopher Janney—or at least his work—in an elevator. (I don't mean this to sound like a joke.) One of Janney's earliest projects, long since gone (it is a particular hazard of the occupation that the buildings and spaces he works with get bought and sold, renovated, or even demolished), was called *Rainbow Pass*. It was an installation in the three elevators of an enclosed shopping emporium in Miami called Miracle Center, designed by the architectural firm Arquitectonica (also early in the firm's career), that created an enveloping, and totally engaging, environmental experience on a very small scale. Janney recorded the hums, words, songs, warbles, whirs, chirps, clicks (and more) of nature in the Florida Everglades and underwater and then programmed the elevators to incorporate those sounds into their own aural ecosystems. The experience was quite amazing, and, as an observer of architecture and of the way in which people and places interact, I found myself riding the elevators just to watch the reactions of those doing so for the first time.

Rainbow Pass, Miracle Center, Coral Gables, Florida, 1989.

Like Janney's first project, *Soundstair* (the work that began as his thesis at the Massachusetts Institute of Technology's Center for Advanced Visual Studies), *Rainbow Pass* presaged his later and more complex works. *Soundstair* involved the application of musical sensors on steps, allowing passersby and participants to "play" (quite literally) the stairs, a concept that evolved as Janney took it on tour to various locations in the United States and Europe, most legendarily Rome's Spanish Steps.

Soundstair was an event, one that people consciously chose to travel to, or happily stumbled upon, and it had a specific time frame; *Rainbow Pass* was much more of an inevitability for shoppers or gym-goers at the Miami Miracle Center. Yet even if one were to consider them precursors, or harbingers, of the work to come, these were dramatic and, one might note, novel interpretations of otherwise everyday experiences. They also set a standard for the kind of unexpected subtlety that marks Janney's work.

Soundstair On Tour, New Music America Festival, Minneapolis, Minnesota, with Nancy Hauser Dance Company, 1981.

Whether the interaction is planned or unexpected, an encounter with one of Janney's large-scale installations (his Urban Musical Instruments, in particular) is intended to enhance our understanding of both time and place, transforming us from observers into participants who encounter his work and its setting, pause to listen as once random and cacophonic sounds become ordered, and delight in the spontaneity of it all. If his theory is rooted in history, Janney's practice offers us a kind of sociology of space, in which our understanding of the immediate and larger (often also metaphysical) context is made acute. Among the earliest of these was *Sonic Forest,* first designed for the Three Rivers Arts Festival in Pittsburgh, and executed on an otherwise bleak plaza in front of Philip Johnson's PPG building. Janney once called it "performance architecture," and that phrase is fitting, with several possible meanings attached. There is the

Sonic Forest, Bonnaroo Music & Arts Festival, Manchester, Tennessee, 2005.

actual performance—music of some sort, or an array of mnemonic sounds culled from actual and archival sources—along with a show of color and light. And there is the fact that the "son et lumière" is only available to those who interact with the work.

Janney's imagination is fertile enough that this takes place in a variety of ways, and though many of his Urban Musical Instruments appear to be members of the same family, with sibling-like similarities, in many cases, they also each bear distinct identities.

Thus, Janney's cladding for the Seventh Street Station in Charlotte, North Carolina—a project entitled *Touch My Building*—involves a syncopated pattern of more than 400 colored panels arranged on the building's nine-story facade. These—together with thirty-six colored-glass fins that fully animate if a passerby solves the "riddle"—might have a kinship to *Light Waves,* installed in 2001 on the facade of the Orlando Public Library, where in addition to the "light show" of colored-glass and neon banners suspended from the front of the building, there is another riddle to solve. Even those pieces that rely on blatant color and large-scale geometries might, on the surface, appear to be more obvious than they actually are upon closer inspection.

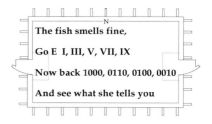

Riddle for *Touch My Building*, Charlotte, North Carolina, 1997.

As Janney's work has evolved over the past three decades, it has grown more complex. Part of this is artistic maturity and an ever-increasing and profound understanding of materials. With experience and practice, he has devised new and innovative ways to integrate an array of sensory experiences into his tangible, physical work. If one traces the evolution of Janney's projects, a greater sophistication emerges. Though some of Janney's earlier projects—*Soundstair,* again, is one such example—explore the world using primarily "constructed sound"; others are far less singular in approach, intertwining architecture, music, light, and color.

There is another aspect to the evolution. The work also relies on the support derived from electrical and mechanical engineering, and the ways in which technology—ranging from ever more sophisticated computers to programmable photoelectric cells—can be harnessed in service of an idea. The decades since 1978 have borne witness to enormous change in both materials and technology, the latter evolving at unanticipated speed. Compare the rudimentary *Soundstair* with Janney's highly complex work two decades later—be it *Turn Up the Heat,* the multimedia "scoreboard" for Miami's NBA basketball team, or one of several "passageways" in airports and institutions like Lehman College in New York, where Janney installed his lush *Sonic Pass Blue.* The refinements and technological improvements continue, so that *Rainbow Cove Green,* in Boston's Logan International Airport, is a more intricate, multi-faceted version of many earlier projects, starting with *Rainbow Pass.* With each iteration of the idea, the execution becomes more sophisticated.

Turn Up the Heat, interactive scoreboard, American Airlines Arena, Miami, 2000.

Janney calls such installations "synaesthetic," largely because there is no way they can be experienced in only one aspect or in a single dimension. This was true, too, of *Harmonic Runway*—installed in the Miami International Airport in 1995 and then tragically, and stupidly, removed (in a kowtow to American Airlines) in 2004 and 2005—in which one walked through a rainbow of colored glass, enveloped in multihued light and sounds recorded underwater and in the Florida Everglades. Janney does not repeat himself, however, and thus *Sonic Pass*

Harmonic Runway, Miami International Airport, 1995.

Blue is highly differentiated from the now-disassembled *Harmonic Runway,* and from another such passageway, called *Passing Light,* which is installed on a 380-foot, five-story "paseo" in the San Antonio International Airport. This latter project offers a case in point in that it is not only a processional but also, with its vivid colors reminiscent of a fiesta day, a celebration of Texas culture. A sundial etched in the floor marks the passage of time.

Sidereal Time, Lexington, Massachusetts, 2001.

The passage of time, the rising and setting of the sun (and moon), and other celestial events have always been part of the making of music (think of the music of the spheres) and, in early days, part of architecture as well. The union of music and architecture brings Janney back to those kinds of cosmic considerations. One sees this particularly in the house he designed for John Ryan in Kona, Hawaii (see page 108), where the house is not only designed as a full-fledged sensory experience but is also based on cosmological principles, as well as the rhythms of the islands. The house, which was completed in 2002, is at once attuned to the movements of the spheres and to its own setting. It features a Steinway piano that plays (by itself) at sunrise, noon, sunset, and midnight, and a clock (there is a second of these in Janney's own home) that charts the position of the sun and moon. The house is thoroughly modern and yet pays full homage to the building vernacular of Hawaii; it is a fully realized exposition of the ideas that Janney has developed over the years, which is not to say that it is a culmination of any sort, but rather a benchmark in a continuing career.

Janney's life, in many ways, follows a seamless whole—from his Washington, D.C., childhood, in which his creative spirit and sense of adventure were nurtured, to his Princeton education, which was at once rigorous and energizing. The late 1960s were a heady time to be a college student, particularly in the arts, where new ideas were fomenting at a furious pace. The end of the sixties and the beginning of the 1970s were a time when traditions were toppled and anything seemed possible; it was a perfect time for the Christopher Janneys of this world. Like many venturesome artists, he was always capable of asking the two—often mutually exclusive—questions, "Why?" and "Why not?," and turning the answers into art of one sort or another.

In the real world, this has imbued Janney with a restless intellectual energy that compels him to explore ever-newer frontiers, ever-newer ways to experience space. Projects such as *HeartBeat* show that we can see space by watching a dancer explore it and, at the same time, that we can understand our inner rhythms by listening to a heart beat. I was fortunate enough to see Mikhail Baryshnikov in *HeartBeat:mb,* and I can only say that it was enthralling. In a way, it was an exercise in the simplest of logical steps, a set of syllogisms transformed into a performance: the heart beats like a drum; therefore, it can become a drum; a dancer can dance to the rhythms of his own body; therefore, it can become choreography. If A, then B... It expands our sense of the possible.

HeartBeat:mb, Mikhail Baryshnikov, New York City, 1999.

But there is an important sociological and demographic consideration here, as well. Janney came of age in an era when Americans were just starting to rediscover the cities so many had grown to spurn in the rush to suburbia that began after World War II and continued for decades. Numerous forces had begun to converge by the mid 1970s. A generation of "baby boomers," who were not satisfied with the proscribed lives of their parents (this is, of course, an egregious oversimplification), began to explore alternatives in art and music, as well as almost every other aspect of life. It was an invigorating time to be in those fields, especially for those in what might be called the "post-Beat" world of New York or the San Francisco Bay area.

At the same time, it was a low moment for urban America. Massive urban renewal projects had left entire chunks of city centers without their natural rhythms, without their innate vibrance. The more noble experiments of modernism had devolved into a kind of formulaic, blank-faced, curtain-wall building that proliferated throughout cities. The mass migration, after World War II, to the suburbs had taken its toll as well, in the form of urban disinvestment. With the urban riots of the 1960s and early 1970s, and the publication of such seminal books as Jane Jacobs's *The Death and Life of Great American Cities,* architects and planners were growing to realize the mistakes of the recent past. As planners struggled to relearn more basic tenets of urbanism, they also sought ways to repair their mistakes. The process was a slow one—the values of the 1950s were entrenched then, and in many ways still are—but one approach was to try to mitigate the impact with an array of urban interventions that ranged from landscaping to art.

All of this is by way of saying that there was not a straight path to what we now think of as the public art movement in America; rather, it was a combination of the renewed, and often experimental, urban art scene in convergence with any number of other forces. The impulses were both positive and what one might regard as negative, or at least remedial, though whatever the motivation, the result was that large-scale contemporary art came into its own in the American public place.

Public—or civic, as some prefer to call it—art was not new in this country, nor in history. From ancient Greece to the Renaissance and beyond, cities were adorned with homages to gods or kings or the victorious in battle— from monumental statues to triumphal arches to the sculptural adornment of civic buildings. We know so many of these today as the landmarks of great cities—the Parthenon in Athens, the Arc de Triomphe in Paris, the Piazza Navona in Rome—and as the adornments of Western European towns, north to south, large to small. The embellished city of the past was one to be seen and admired and cherished, and, to be sure, it has endured.

But in the New World—with its vast and often unaccommodating lands, its fast-growing cities, its enduring practicalities—the adorned city was more elusive; the rules of the Renaissance were not to be applied, especially as cities became modern in the twentieth and twenty-first centuries. This is, admittedly, a gross generalization. One can point to any number of elegant squares and plazas, fountains and facades in American cities, but it is safe to say that, particularly in the mid and late twentieth century, these niceties of urban architecture were less than appreciated. It was a particular time in this country's development.

The modern public art movement has its roots in the alphabet-soup programs of the Great Depression—in the Works Progress Administration and its murals, in the Civilian Conservation Corps and its sculpture, and more. These "make-work" programs were intended to shore up a bleak economy and provide subsistence in the form of employment and income for artists; they also provided us with a rich artistic legacy and documentation of the period. The WPA art programs did not, necessarily, break with the past; even if the work itself was not

Pruitt-Igoe housing development being demolished, Saint Louis, Missouri, 1972.

Classical Greek sculpture.

WPA artists work on a backdrop for a theater production, New York City, 1935.

traditional, it adorned buildings and other structures in the centuries-old fashion—as murals, friezes, and sculpture.

It was not until decades later that public art began to speak for itself. By the 1970s, many municipalities (as well as some state governments and federal agencies) began enacting "percent for art" programs. These programs set aside a certain percentage (usually just one or two) for artwork, and the selection process became arduous, with panels of experts examining slides and reading proposals for work to be incorporated into new buildings and plazas.

The impetus for all this was severalfold. First, and probably foremost, was to create a sense of place where little existed and to adorn otherwise bleak governmental buildings and plazas, the product of architecture's least felicitous (and one might argue, most cynical) era. Though its roots lie in the movements of the early twentieth century (among them the Vienna Secessionists), modernism was born in the thriving artistic era between the two world wars, most particularly at the Bauhaus (formed in Berlin but relocated to the town of Dessau, just outside of the city), and was ultimately imported to America as architects and artists fled Nazi oppression.

The Bauhaus, Dessau, Germany, 1925.

Those early years were a time of enormous intellectual ferment, powerful and stimulating. The excitement transferred from Europe to America, where, at first, a number of the Bauhaus refugees found an initial home at Black Mountain College, near Asheville, North Carolina. However, by the time World War II was over, the stars of the Bauhaus had scattered—Walter Gropius and Marcel Breuer to Harvard, Josef and Anni Albers to Yale, Mies van der Rohe first to Harvard and then to the Illinois Institute of Technology. The work was in pursuit of a utopian ideal and a certain aesthetic perfection—all of which was achieved.

As time went on, though, the ideas and ideals of the movement went astray. The reductive nature of modernism made it possible for van der Rohe to design the Farnsworth House in Plano, Illinois, but also the high-rise Seagram Building in New York; it yielded the Glass House of Philip Johnson and the Lever House, by Skidmore, Owings & Merrill. Fine buildings followed, but along the way, the ideas began to be corrupted into a kind of base commercialism that filled city streets with bland and faceless buildings towering over barren plazas. This, then, became the context of America's public art program.

Faculty at Black Mountain College, Asheville, North Carolina, 1951.

Bauhaus was, of course, not the only impetus. The same era (more productive for art than for architecture, ultimately) produced a generation of artists working not just at a larger scale, but with new materials and techniques compatible with the oversize world of buildings. The opportunities for collaboration between artists and architects were legion—enough so that, by 1980, the Architectural League of New York commemorated its centennial with an exhibition (it later traveled to museums across the country) that celebrated a number of renowned architect-and-artist partnerships. Many of those featured in *Collaborations: Artists and Architects* had such powerful connections that they seemed almost inevitable—Frank Stella and Richard Meier, for example.

But not all public art endeavors were quite so successful. Richard Serra's *Tilted Arc,* created for Federal Plaza in New York City, was greeted with accolades by the critics and with emotions ranging from derision to downright hatred by the building's users and visitors; it was eventually removed. Serra is a brilliant sculptor, and one is tempted to defend *Tilted Arc* solely on high moral grounds, yet there is an object lesson to be learned from its general reception. That is to say that public art—as opposed to art made for its own sake or done as a private commission—has a difficult path to follow, one that bridges comprehension and culture without compromising the creator. This has provoked no shortage of controversy over the years. How does a public body—in most cases, an appointed panel or governmental agency—allow for artistic integrity and encourage creativity, while at the same time meeting the expectations of a less anointed, less erudite public? It is often a slippery slope, and yet, ultimately, in a reach beyond their own scope of experience, many Americans will begin to appreciate and understand the complexities of art.

Richard Serra, *Tilted Arc*, Federal Plaza, New York City, 1981.

It is in this context that one must look at Janney's work. Intriguingly, though his muses (both in music and in the visual arts) are modern, his understanding of cities and spaces—as well as his deep understanding of the ways in which music and sound are integrated into civic life—draws on a variety of historical precedents.

His study of glockenspiels in town squares and plazas in central European villages and cities provides an important example. Integrated into the architecture and the townscape and yet set apart by function, the glockenspiel is both practical and fanciful—it functions pragmatically as the timekeeper for a populace but far more poetically as entertainment, diversion, and art. Janney's own glockenspiel—part of his *Sonic Plaza* at East Carolina University in Greenville, North Carolina—hearkens to the historic precedent. The clock tower element, called the Media Glockenspiel, is an eighty-five-foot structure culminating in a timepiece, but at its base is a circular ring of video monitors that are changeable. The idea was to let students (under supervision) program the images. The plaza itself has preexisting classical columns that Janney manipulated so that a visitor, on arriving, triggers photoelectric cells that in turn activate a litany of sounds—both melodic and environmental. Both of these elements, which are two of Janney's four interventions in this particular plaza (the others include a percussive Water Wall and a Ground Cloud of mist that emanates from a twelve-foot grate), draw from classic historic precedents but are transformed as contemporary iterations.

Glockenspiel, Prague, fifteenth century.

Media Glockenspiel, East Carolina University, Greenville, North Carolina, 1996.

Janney's Princeton education—at once imbued with the rigor of tradition and yet progressively modern—serves him well in projects such as these. The work rings with familiarity brought on by centuries of civic building projects, but still is entirely novel. This is important, as it means that the work resonates within a collective memory but also intrigues and tantalizes with its unexpected twists.

This duality enriches Janney's work. It is explicit in projects like his own house in Lexington, Massachusetts, where he designed an addition to a rather plain 1920s farmhouse. The addition faces the street with comparative modesty, looking somewhat like a modernist structure of the same time period, but becomes far more radical as one steps back. Janney eschews delicacy and detailing, preferring to make a strong statement; the work might even be considered outspoken, certainly neither modest nor subtle. But that is part of the point. Aptly, since he is also a drummer, Janney's design is to architecture what percussion is to music—unmistakably powerful and, at the same time, surprising in the nuances contained within those bold strokes.

Janney's home, Lexington, Massachusetts, 2003.

Much of the controversy over public art in the last decades has derived from the public perception that this form of art was devoid of meaning. "Plop art," as it came to be called, got its name because it was thought to have been art made without any site specificity—without any comprehensible connection to time, place, or local custom or culture. Janney's work, even at its most abstract, avoids this. It is always connected, whether to its larger setting or, more directly, to the particular architecture of which it is a part. The latter is more often the case in projects that involve some form of passage, such as those in an airport concourse or an elevator, where the intervention becomes part of the architecture, and the experience of the art and the experience of the place become inextricably intertwined.

In that respect, Janney's work shares much in common with that of Christo and Jeanne-Claude, whose Central Park installation, *The Gates*, attracted worldwide attention in 2005. There are numerous differences, clearly: Christo and Jeanne-Claude finance their art through the sale of private work leading up to a public project, for starters. Further, Christo's work is temporal (which is sometimes the case for Janney, but not always). Both work toward the same goal, which is to enhance the viewer's understanding and perception, to tantalize the senses and, in so doing, to tell us more about art, architecture, landscape, and history.

The late and much-lamented *Harmonic Runway*—now gone from the Miami International Airport after an ill-conceived master plan proffered by American Airlines was put into effect there—is a case in point. At first impression, it seemed little more than large-scale, colored-glass panels, attractive in their own right; but then the nuances of the installation took over. What did it mean? Was it a rainbow to walk through, as Janney conceived it? Once the sound and the inevitable interplay of light were added, it became a full-flush sensory experience, one that welcomed arriving passengers and bid farewell to those leaving on what were usually lengthy (as it was an international concourse) journeys, at the same time imparting an idea of the brilliant color, light, and melodic sounds of the subtropics, of South Florida.

The experience is enhanced in so many of Janney's projects by his deep understanding of local conditions—history, culture, literature, nature. Though his work was launched with *Soundstair,* which Janney has transported across the country and to Europe (other "portable" projects, such as *Sonic Forest,* also look to the general idea of public spaces and how they are used), many others have a site specificity ranging from the oblique to the obvious.

In Miami again, Janney's scoreboard for the Miami Heat's American Airlines Arena is a case in point. On one level, it may seem an abstraction, a work of contemporary sculpture. On another, it suggests the otherworldly forms found deep in the ocean, or possibly (taking it to yet a third level of interpretation), a flight of imagination. It is at once a part of the place and apart from it, most particularly at triumphant moments when the scoreboard is transformed into a fireworks display. The National Steamboat Monument in Cincinnati, titled *Whistle Grove,* shows Janney's profound sense of the juxtaposition of the abstract and the specific, the familiar and the unfamiliar. In many ways, it is the consummate expression of his ideas. The form—twenty-four stainless steel "smokestacks"—is familiar but unique in that, like *Sonic Forest,* the columns sit on a plaza, luring visitors to wander through as if in the woods. Two taller columns hold up an

Henry Moore, *Reclining Connected Forms,* 1969 (top), Christo and Jeanne-Claude, *The Gates,* Central Park, New York City, 2005 (bottom).

A giant green sea anemone.

Turn Up the Heat, interactive scoreboard, American Airlines Arena, Miami, 2000.

actual retired paddle wheel from a steamboat. The "message"—in the form of recordings of whistles, calliopes, and archival narrations by rivermen and boat captains—is historical, but all this occurs in a larger context of the contemporary. There is a riddle to answer, lights that can be triggered, and modern music to hear. Even with these playful features, *Whistle Grove* is extremely contextual, with its array of historical and geographical references.

The indoor labyrinth in Grace Cathedral, San Francisco.

The ideas of processionals and passages are as old as architecture itself, perfected by the Greeks and never really bettered since. Processionals assume an utmost importance in the kind of work Janney so often does, as his work is ultimately experiential, requiring participation and engagement, whether visual, auditory, intellectual, or a combination of all three. The process begins at a distance, at which point it is almost entirely visual, and then evolves, with new dimensions emerging as one draws closer. A project like *Sonic Gates: Manchester* draws on the age-old ideas of arrival and procession, with the addition of a sound-score, activated as one passes between two of the columns (the score is described by Janney as "a mix of melodic and environmental sounds"), and, again, a riddle to solve. The gates were built as the entrance to the library at Manchester Community College, in Manchester, Connecticut. Lighted columns hold up a circular tower piece that is the main focus of the building's architecture, and though the building is modernist, an entrance rotunda like this one has deep roots in architectural history—though historically, such columnated gateways were without the electronic bells and whistles.

Sonic Gates: Manchester, Manchester Community College, Manchester, Connecticut, 2000.

What is so fascinating about Janney's work is its strong connection to primordial antecedents and to centuries of urban tradition, yet it is thoroughly contemporary. Each of his pieces has been done in a way that ties the work to the most ancient of sources—the shamans of mankind's tribal past, for example—while expressing ideas in a modern, if not contemporary, fashion. The inspiration found in primitive cultures wends its way forward through history in the often-parallel paths of music and architecture. Janney draws from observations of the world, too—in particular, from the great cities of Europe, where there has always been a layering of meaning that renders them at once mysterious and yet ultimately easy to comprehend.

His observations are sometimes empirical, but just as often they derive from emotion or intuition or a purely visceral understanding of the world around us. The interesting thing is that the work seldom fully exists without public participation to animate it. Like the engaging riddles that Janney offers, this is a conundrum in and of itself: Is art actually art with no beholder? Art and music, sound and light, have always been communal acts. Throughout history, they have offered forms of conversation, of communication, but there is more. Art and music express a society's mores, its beliefs, its culture; where two or more are gathered, there is always the opportunity to make music, to make art.

A shaman with ceremonial drum, Russia.

It is the particular genius of Janney's work that he evokes in us the shared memories of generations, some of which are specific to a time or place and others of which are far more universal. Janney talks of finding the "hidden music" in architecture, and indeed, his work *does* make the built environment come alive in ways that speak not just to our five senses but also to our hearts and souls.

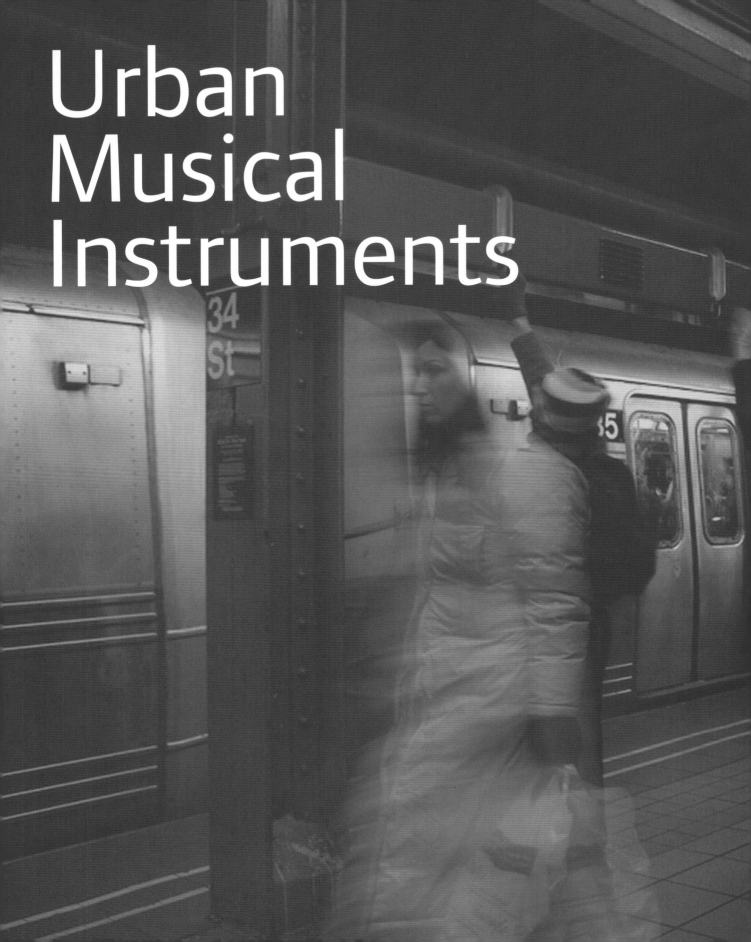

Urban
Musical
Instruments

Soundstair
1979-Present
Soundstair On Tour: 1979-1991
Soundstair: Boston, 1988
Soundstair: Minnesota, 1990
Soundstair: Columbia, South Carolina
Soundstair: Patent #4,404,933, 3/12/85

The genesis for Janney's Urban Musical Instrument series was *Soundstair*, his first major interactive project to combine the elements of music and architecture. The seeds for *Soundstair* were planted in 1978 at the Massachussetts Institute of Technology, where Janney was working toward his master's degree in environmental art under Otto Piene in the architecture school (Piene was the director of MIT's Center for Advanced Visual Studies from 1974 to 1994). Janney found MIT to be fertile ground for his early investigations into art that goes beyond the confines of the studio.

Looking for a sound-space he could commandeer, Janney was offered a fourth-floor stairway in the architecture building at MIT. Here he was able to work out the concepts and technology required for the first, admittedly home-made, version of *Soundstair* (including off-the-shelf parts from Radio Shack)—a version Janney concedes was "a mess that sounded awful." Yet this first attempt was successful enough to show Janney that the project had viable future possibilities. His idea of creating an interactive sound stairway, transforming a transitional space into a place of destination with sound, as well as using sound to "paint a space with a palette of ever-changing colors," was indeed possible.

Janney knew that he would need help on the engineering side of things (after all, he was a musician and an architect, not an electrical engineer), so he turned to Robert Dezmelyk, a former bass player who was an electrical engineering student at MIT. "When I showed him the prototype, he said, 'You need to build a synthesizer,'" Janney recalls. Realizing that this was out of his sphere of competence, Janney soon found other interested students at MIT who could build according to his specifications. Janney also realized that he was working in a "creative gene pool" where he could find an engineer or a scientist to build literally anything he could imagine. It was his responsibility to formulate and clarify his vision, as well as to inspire and then collaborate with his colleagues to achieve that vision. This was an important lesson to learn during his formative years as a professional designer and artist.

As an artist, Janney was concerned with the integrity of his vision and needed to be able to supervise the construction process as his work moved off the drawing board and into the realm of reality. He agrees with the edict that "art is one percent inspiration and ninety-nine percent perspiration." He puts it quite bluntly: "If you don't have that one percent, you can pack it in. Your ideas must be crystal clear. That initial spark has to have a great deal of potential energy; it must ignite a flame that has to burn into every participating engineer's imagination." As an idea, *Soundstair* was clear enough, and the year after the alpha version, work on the project proceeded. Robert Dezmelyk, the synthesizer engineer, filed for an independent study course to work with Janney on what became Janney's graduate thesis project.

Soundstair was built with stand-alone photo-sensors, one per step, on a staircase. With invisible beams of light running across the stairs and reflected by a mirror back to a receiver, information was sent to a multichannel synthesizer and then on to an amplified speaker system. When the light beams were broken, they triggered a series of sounds. As people went up or down these fourth-floor steps, they were surprised as they set off the unexpected sounds, adding a bit of levity and even unexpected humor to their day. Janney changed the parameters and pitch of the sounds each day, like a street musician playing a very sophisticated musical instrument.

The next year, in 1979, Janney won a commission from the Three Rivers Arts Festival in Pittsburgh, Pennsylvania, to design a large-scale art project for an estimated audience of 200,000 people who would attend the event over four days. "Why not build a version of *Soundstair* that could tour?" he asked himself. Having learned well enough in the MIT environment not to try to reinvent the wheel, Janney conceived of a well-built "roadable" version of *Soundstair*, made from the finest of existing musical and electronic technology on the market. He contacted Rockwell International, one of the only manufacturers of desktop computers at the time (this was 1979), and Oberheim Electronics, the best analog synthesizer manufacturer, as well as others, to assemble the sturdiest components available for the third incarnation of *Soundstair*. As Janney stated, "The piece was slowly but surely moving out of the laboratory, out of the university environment, getting 'legs' of its own, and moving into the real world." Dezmelyk, now familiar with Janney's vision, designed the necessary hardware and software interface to Janney's specifications.

The festival asked Janney if he could devise a performance element to accompany the musical staircase. He suggested a piece by choreographer Martha Armstrong Gray, whose Boston dance company Janney admired. Gray choreographed a piece that would tour with *Soundstair* for several years, with installations/performances straddling the globe, from the National Gallery in Washington, D.C., to the Spanish Steps in Rome. As a musician, Janney's goal was to tour the world, but as an architect, he wanted to make *Soundstair* a permanent part of urban environments. To date, permanent installations have been installed at the Minnesota and Boston Museums of Science, the Mississippi Museum of Art, the South Carolina Aquarium, and Bonds-New York, a prestigious Manhattan night club.

People respond to the discovery of *Soundstair* in different ways. Janney finds that some are curious and amused when they realize what's happening, asking questions like, "What are you doing?" or "What are you selling?" Janney replies, "I try to spark their imagination, sometimes telling them it's part of a psychology experiment, or it's a humor meter, measuring their sense of humor," as he avoids the explanation of environmental art. "People don't expect art outside of a gallery, out in the open."

As *Soundstair* toured the world, Janney found that it was a cultural mirror of sorts, reflecting and amplifying people's personalities: "In Tulsa, Oklahoma, someone remarked that it would make a great burglar alarm. In Essen, Germany, an elderly woman said to me, 'You Americans have no culture, and you never will.'" With responses such as these, Janney began to wonder how successfully he was communicating the essence of his work.

The next stop on the tour was the Piazza di Spania in Rome, the famous Spanish Steps. "I had long admired this site and often dreamed of 'plugging in' *Soundstair* to these stairs," notes Janney. "Based on my analysis of the short attention span in Essen, I said we would follow the same format with short performances interspersed with public interaction. What I had not figured on was the change of culture. The Romans would come, bring their lunch or dinner, and sit on the edge of the steps for three hours! After the first day, one Roman came up to me and said, 'It is a dream for Cinderella.'"

At that moment, Janney had a flash of insight. Comments from "burglar alarm" to "no culture" to "Cinderella" were not comments on his work; they were comments on different cultures. *Soundstair* was a "cultural barometer," he realized. "The piece created its own cultural bubble. I laughed at how it was not just an instrument that transforms architecture, but now it was also an instrument that had transformed me. It was moving, changing, causing sometimes distaste, sometimes fascination, sometimes ambivalence. My travels with *Soundstair* were my vehicle, my instrument to reveal parts of the culture. I was no longer just plugging into architecture; I was plugging into the culture, the Zeitgeist."

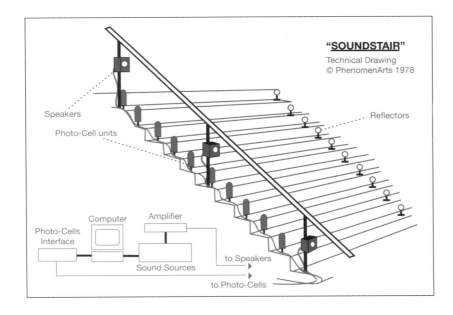

Technical drawing for *Soundstair*, 1978.

Top: *Soundstair: Boston* with the Dance Collective, Martha Armstrong Gray, choreographer, 1979.
Middle: *Soundstair: Minnesota*, New Music America Festival with Nancy Hauser Dance Company, 1981.
Bottom: *Soundstair: Metropolitan Museum of Art*, New York City, Dancing in the Streets Festival, 1990.
Overleaf: *Soundstair: Rome*, 1981.

Touch My Building 1998
Bank of America parking garage Charlotte, North Carolina

Light, colored glass, and sounds transform a 300-by-120-foot, nine-story Bank of America employee parking garage in Charlotte, North Carolina, turning the building into a large-scale environmental artwork that is one of Janney's best-known permanent, site-specific Urban Musical Instruments. Completed in 1998, the project was the result of a closed competition initiated by the bank, in which artists were asked to submit designs that would enhance the look of the entire garage.

The facade of the building is unusual, with 416 aluminum panels painted in custom car colors, such as cherry red and sunburst blue. Sunlight dances off these panels during the day, giving the building a definite shimmer. Janney's goal was not just to enhance the facade but to change the overall perception of the building. While the garage was being designed, he added transparent red glass and neon "taillight fins" onto thirty-six columns. Under Janney's direction, Mystic Scenic of Dedham, Massachusetts, supplied the neon and developed the computer-controlled touch-plate technology. Touching the fins allows pedestrians to interact with the entire structure and "play with" the architecture.

Janney designed *Touch My Building* on two scales: the architectural, using large forms to produce abstract patterns of colored light and shadow; and the pedestrian, attaching at ground level a series of forms that people could touch to trigger a mix of melodic and environmental sounds. When pedestrians interact with the thirty-foot fins, the neon lights up and sounds are heard from nearby speakers in the walls. "You get to light up your fin. This is an attempt to give the passing pedestrian a sense of touching the building, making physical contact with the architecture," says Janney.

One of Janney's inspirations for this project was the architect I. M. Pei's triangular extension to the National Gallery in Washington, D.C. There is a spot where people have touched the wall so many times that it has changed color, giving Janney the idea to design something that people could touch to change the building. For Janney, this helps to give the building a personality, a character, and gets people to develop a relationship with it.

At night, high-intensity discharge (HID) lamps light the entire facade, making the aluminum panels and the neon even more visible. Transparent glass in eight shades of blue, lit with fluorescent tubes, highlights the edges of two open, 110-foot-high staircases (one at each end of the garage). This avoids having the stairs look like dark, monolithic towers. At night, these towers look like city-scale light sculptures anchoring the building. Janney describes them as "big blue monoliths glowing with fluorescence." During the day, Janney counts on the sun as a light source to dance through slabs of colored glass and create colored shadows. Cylindrical holes cut into the pediment around the roof allow light to filter through and throw elliptical shadows on the building's upper surfaces, adding to the festive feel of the structure.

For computer renderings, shadow studies, and animation analyzing the changing color patterns of shadows, Janney was one of the first to use the 3D Studio Max program by Kinetics, a division of Autodesk. The sound/light interface was developed on a Macintosh computer using Opcode's MAX Cycling 74 software. Janney also worked with PAVO Engineering in Seattle to build a custom-designed sampler/synthesizer card as the sound source for the thirty-six touch plates used in *Touch My Building*.

The structure also "performs" on the hour, with the neon lights flashing in computer-triggered patterns. Janney wrote a piece of music that responds to the acoustic bells of a nearby church that also play on the hour. Loudspeakers placed on the fifth story keep the sound in scale with the building.

To add still another layer of experience to the *Touch My Building* idea, Janney built a "riddle" into the design, with a pictogram that tells spectators the order in which they should touch the fins. When someone solves the riddle by touching the fins in the correct order, the lights and sounds chase around the building in a special thirty-second pattern. Since 1998, the riddle has been solved sixty-four times. Janney can check from his studio computer; he has an agreement with the bank that when it has been solved one hundred times, he will write a new riddle. The building is now such an integral part of the Charlotte landscape that its reputation has spread beyond the city's borders, and visitors often stop at the Chamber of Commerce to ask where they can find the "music building with the riddle."

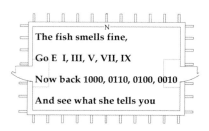

The riddle built into *Touch My Building*. Pedestrians who solve the riddle are rewarded with a light-and-sound performance.

CORNICE —
TOWER —
PANELS —
FINS —

TOWER

CORNICE ORANGE/YELLOW
TOWER BLUE/VIOLET
PANELS BLUE/GREEN
FINS- VIOLET/RED

NOT solid color -
like brush strokes
pointillist

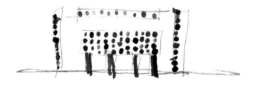

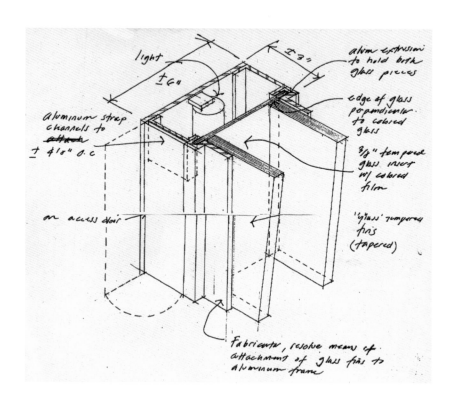

light
± 6"
± 3"

alum extrusion
to hold both
glass pieces

aluminum strap
channels to
attach
± 4'0" o.c.

edge of glass
perpendicular
to colored
glass

3/8" tempered
glass insert
w/ colored
film

"glass" tempered
fins
(tapered)

on access door

Fabricate, resolve means of
attachment of glass fins to
aluminum frame

Top: Color study for fin patterns.
Bottom: Construction detail for the
illuminated fin.

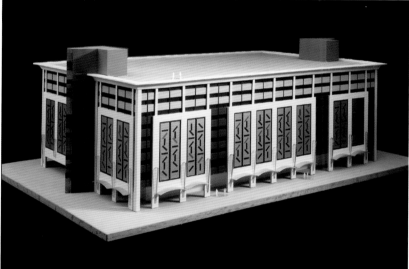

Top: *Touch My Building*, 1998 sketch.
Middle: One-sixteenth-inch scale model.
Bottom: Computer rendering.
Overleaf: Southwest facade of bank parking
structure (left) and detail of interactive touch
panel (right).

Reach: New York
1997
34th Street/Herald Square
Subway station, New York City

Passengers waiting for the N and R trains on the subway platforms at 34th Street/Herald Square in New York City may notice something unusual about this station: Travelers on the opposite platform may begin behaving strangely, waving their arms in the air for no apparent reason, while sounds from places definitely not New York fill the space. The gritty, industrial character of this subway station provided Janney with the perfect environment for *Reach: New York*, one of his interactive Urban Musical Instruments, artworks that bring a sense of celebration to unexpected places.

Installed along the platforms of the BMT Broadway line at 34th Street in Manhattan in 1996, *Reach: New York* has the potential to reach a large audience on a daily basis. The 34th Street/Herald Square station is, in fact, the third busiest in the entire subway system, serving the IND Sixth Avenue line, the BMT Broadway line, and the PATH line that goes to and from New Jersey, with commuters streaming through from early morning until well into the evening. An estimated 112,000 passengers walk along these platforms each week. Even in this chaotic environment, the simplicity of the *Reach: New York* concept means that the project remains virtually maintenance-free.

The idea for this underground installation is a variation on the theme of one of Janney's earlier works, *Soundstair*, which also used photoelectric cells, or "electric eyes," to trigger music and sounds via computer. Before the idea for a piece along a subway platform evolved, Janney had been wondering how to incorporate the technology he had developed for the stairways of *Soundstair* into another architectural space. He was exploring the idea of a hallway where the photo-sensors would be placed just high enough overhead for people to wave their arms and activate the "instrument." This idea became *Reach: New York*, where Janney adds an artistic experience and a bit of curious experimentation to the commuter's everyday life.

Janney developed the prototype for this long lineup of photo-sensors while he was a research fellow at MIT. The first iterations of this piece were temporary installations in three different locations in three countries: the Boston subway, the Paris metro, and the entrance tunnel to a building in Linz, Austria, as part of the 1980 Ars Electronica Festival. A soundscape was triggered as people came in and out of the building.

After the success of the temporary versions in the underground passages of Boston and Paris, the idea was conjured once again when the New York City Metropolitan Transit Authority called Janney to discuss ideas for an installation. In *Reach: New York*, the photoelectric cells are hung inside an aluminum tube along the subway platforms on both sides of the tracks. The sensors shine an invisible beam of light above the heads of waiting passengers, who can raise their arms and trigger sound anywhere within the platform area. People waiting on the other side can respond by waving their arms in return.

As the commuters reach up, they break the beams of light and trigger the music computer, eliciting sounds, from melodic instruments like marimbas and flutes to "sound images" of exotic environments like the Florida Everglades or the Brazilian rain forest. The passengers on each side not only can play the "instrument" among themselves, but are also able to interact with others across the tracks.

The principal sponsor for *Reach: New York* is Origins, the body and skin-care company whose philosophy emphasizes all-natural products. The company was interested in Janney's project because of the way he juxtaposes sound images of natural places with the man-made, underground subway environment, to calming, slightly surreal, effect.

Reach: New York is yet another example of how Janney reinvents the way urban environments are perceived, from public plazas to subway stations. "I am interested in using art to elevate the quality of everyday life. I'm not interested in removing a person from reality, as in watching television or playing a virtual reality game. I am interested in creating a hyperreality—a place where a person is still aware of being in his normal environment, but elements of it have been heightened or altered—to invite a more interesting daily experience, as well as to push against the idea of urban alienation," he explains. "*Reach: New York* illustrates this concept, particularly in this tense, underground, man-made setting."

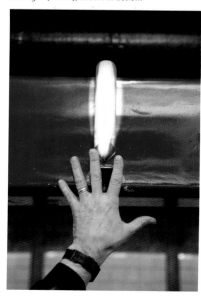

Opposite and below: Details of photo-sensor and light (below), shown in action.

Opposite, left, and overleaf: Passengers interact with *Reach: New York* along the 34th Street/Herald Square subway platform.

Sonic Plaza
1997
East Carolina University
Greenville, North Carolina

In 1991, Janney was selected as the artist on a design team to design an outdoor plaza at East Carolina University in Greenville, North Carolina. He had not been asked to propose a scheme for the project but had been selected on the basis of his portfolio to date and an interview. Janney's training as an architect enabled him to discuss design concepts with the other members of the creative team, headed by architect Larry Robbs, principal of the Winston-Salem firm Walter Robbs Callahan. The result is a seamless integration of art and architecture within *Sonic Plaza*.

A series of interactive installations, *Sonic Plaza* has four distinct elements integrated into the landscape of a 300-foot-long plaza that stretches between the interior of the college campus and a city street, transforming an open space into an intriguing work of art. Janney's work was commissioned by the North Carolina Arts Council under the Artworks for State Buildings program and was completed in 1997.

At one end, a person enters *Sonic Plaza* through the *Sonic Gates,* a series of four white marble Doric columns topped with a horizontal lintel. Now freestanding, the columns once graced the facade of the original Joyner Library building that is now located elsewhere on the plaza. Without changing the look of the columns, Janney turned a classical architectural element into an interactive, postmodern sculpture, hiding photo-sensors in the columns and embedding loudspeakers in the lintel. People walking through the gates trigger random patterns of melodic and environmental sounds, signaling their arrival and departure.

A large-scale water feature, *Percussion Water Wall,* is the second element one encounters while walking along *Sonic Plaza*. The landscape architect had specified a location for a large water feature on a wall to mask the cacophonic sounds from a nearby mechanical services area. Janney suggested that he animate the water. As a result, sixty-five water jets, arranged in thirteen rows of

Sonic Gates: East Carolina University, Greenville, North Carolina, 1997.

Geometric pattern on *Percussion Water Wall*.

five, splash choreographed, computerized patterns of "water mushrooms" (fixtures also designed by Janney) onto the fifteen-by-forty-foot wall.

Continuing along the plaza, one comes to Janney's *Media Glockenspiel*. Robbs had designed an eighty-five-foot clock tower as a central architectural element and new campus icon. At the time, Janney was interested in the concept of glockenspiels, especially a fifteenth-century example he had encountered in Prague. "A glockenspiel is like an 'urban performance,' where something happens every hour," notes Janney. "People gather around to watch and then go on their way."

Adding media to his contemporary glockenspiel, Janney placed a dozen twenty-two-inch video monitors on the face of the clock, replacing the positions of the traditional numbers. In the center is a three-foot-square set of doors that opens four times a day, with various sculptures appearing: at dawn, a copper collage of a rooster pops out, with an accompanying early-morning "cock-a-doodle-doo"; at noon, an untidy heap of old brass trumpets, trombones, and tubas appears, accompanied by twelve sounds from a brass ensemble; at sunset, a cannon, complete with "smoke" (actually, theatrical fog) and a firing sound effect, evokes the pirate mascot of the school; and at midnight, a joker makes an appearance, together with an excerpt from Shakespeare's *Richard II* on "fleeting time."

All of the sculptures were contributed by students from various university art departments, as Janney wanted to get the student body involved in the creative process and give them a sense of ownership in the work. In fact, he worked with the dance, media, and sculpture departments, giving students the chance to choreograph patterns for the water on the percussive wall via independent study courses. The head of the media department, Carl Twarog, built a small, working mock-up of the *Media Glockenspiel* in a classroom and asked his students to design media for the video monitors. For Janney, this process provided "a laboratory for interested students—the school instituted a competition to design new sculptures and media content."

Finally, one encounters the fourth element, *Sonic Plaza: Ground Cloud*, an illuminated mist fountain. This twelve-foot, circular fountain emits a cloud of water vapor, which responds to the wind and the movement of people walking by. Illuminated from sunset to sunrise by thousand-watt, waterproof PAR (parabolic aluminized reflector) lamps located in the fountain, the cloud dances at various speeds and densities, depending on the weather.

Sonic Plaza reflects Janney's fascination with technology and employs photoelectric cells and sophisticated video-switching systems to make the interaction possible via multiple computers located in the base of the clock tower. Sophisticated animation software allows for the display of kinetic images, such as one-twelfth of a bicycle wheel on each monitor, adding up to a giant wheel spinning on the face of the clock.

The four separate elements of *Sonic Plaza* are spaced far enough apart to create a series of individual experiences. A Webcam (http://www.ecu.edu/ecu/onlocation.cfm?B) allows anyone on campus, or any place else in the world, to see what's happening on *Sonic Plaza* at any time of the day or night.

Prague glockenspiel, fifteenth century.

Brain center: the computer room for *Media Glockenspiel* and *Percussion Water Wall*.

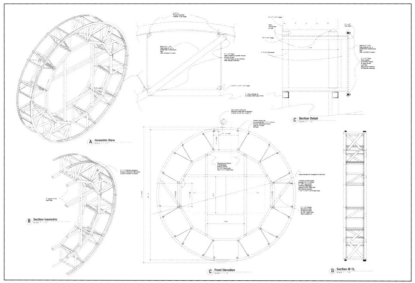

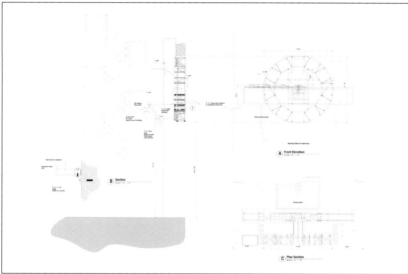

Top and center: Construction drawings for *Media Glockenspiel*.
Bottom: Custom designed software interface for *Media Glockenspiel*.

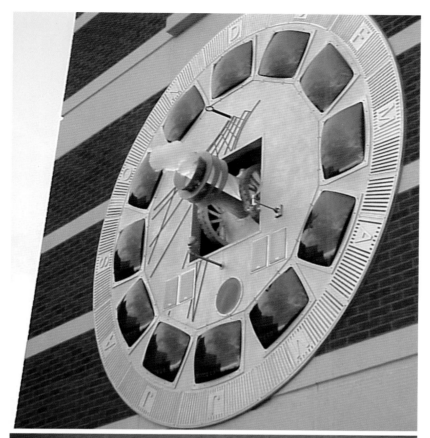

Top: The *Media Glockenspiel* cannon fires at sunset.

Bottom: Twelve video monitors display graphic patterns from sunset to sunrise.

Page 44: *Percussion Water Wall* with student dance/music performance, 1998 (top). *Ground Cloud*, night view (bottom).

Page 45: Daytime view of the plaza.

Whistle Grove: The National Steamboat Monument 2002
Cincinnati, Ohio

In response to a design competition for the National Steamboat Monument in Cincinnati, Ohio, Janney turned to the iconography of the golden age of steamboats, juxtaposing high-tech smokestacks with an authentic riverboat paddle wheel to create one of his large, outdoor, multisensory musical instruments. This permanent, site-specific installation sits along one bank of the Ohio River, a primary artery for the shipping of manufactured goods to points both south and west in the mid-nineteenth century, and was jointly funded by the Cincinnati Recreation Commission and the Greater Cincinnati Tall Stacks Commission.

Embracing both nostalgia for life on the great American rivers and the role of the steamboat in the nation's history, twenty-four ten-foot, stainless steel towers evoke the smokestacks of a ship: when visitors move through the "grove," they activate steam jets in the towers, and steam pours out of the top. Above the smokestacks sits the original thirty-foot-diameter, three-story, bright red paddle wheel from the *American Queen*, a steamship launched in 1995, the largest overnight passenger vessel built by a U.S. shipyard since the 1950s. The sixty-ton wheel was replaced on the ship by a smaller, more efficient one, making this authentic piece of Americana available to Janney. It was donated by the Delta Queen Steamboat Company.

Proximity-sensing photocells are placed inside the towers. These trigger steam solenoids to open and close the steam valves, creating the first layer of interaction. When visitors walk past the columns, they trigger not only the bursts of steam but also an environmental soundtrack that adds the second layer of interaction. The sound-score composed by Janney includes music from a calliope, voices of men loading ships, stories by old riverboat captains, passages from Mark Twain's classic, *The Adventures of Huckleberry Finn*, and steamboat whistles, all overlapping to form what Janney calls "a sonic portrait of an era." The sounds are heard through a series of twenty-four custom-designed, sixty-watt loudspeakers, one per smokestack, that Janney designed for the project: a gigantic surround-sound system.

In researching the sound clips, Janney relied on the knowledge of a local historian and visited an historical archive, where he found vintage tapes of steamboat captains telling tales about life on the river. He hired musicians to record Negro spirituals popular in the nineteenth century and actors to read passages from *Huckleberry Finn*. The ever-changing mix of sound and steam differs for every visitor, giving each individual an immediate, personal experience, a living collage steeped in historical atmosphere.

Steamshuffle: interactive steam, sound, glass, text installation created with Joan Brigham, Philadelphia 1982.

Janney's intention is that the soundtrack should communicate a sense of what life was like on the river at the height of its commercial importance, from the daily hardships to the moments of peacefulness. Since the installation is open twenty-four hours a day, lights come on after dark, wrapping the clouds of steam in a layer of illumination and adding a new dimension at night. The lights are both blue industrial aircraft landing lights—or, more precisely LED (light-emitting diode) lights—and PAR 20 (parabolic aluminized reflector) lamps pointing up into the steam. The lights, the loudspeakers (a custom audio interface with four six-channel amplifiers), and the steam valves are all controlled by an Apple G4 Macintosh computer located in a control room 300 feet from the smokestacks. Also housed there is what Janney calls "a big mother steam boiler." The entire control system is linked via modem to Janney's studio outside of Boston.

The properties of steam appeal to Janney: "It's so visual. And the colder it gets, the thicker the steam gets. It's like a microenvironment you can control." Yet the valves don't envelop those walking through in steam. Rather, it wafts above their heads, like a cloud, as they play among the smokestacks. For Janney, who understood how steam worked and was interested in designing an interactive steam/sound fountain, this project seemed tailor-made.

Steam Beat: interactive steam, sound, performance with Joan Brigham and J. Galeota, 1983.

Whistle Grove can also be played as a twenty-four-note musical instrument, with each smokestack acting as a note. In an eleven-minute piece scored by Janney and the saxophone player Stan Strickland, the breath of a musician playing an electronic wind instrument triggers the steam jets in any combination, from one at a time to all twenty-four in unison. Acoustic brass players (tuba, trombone, and two trumpets) stroll through the grove as part of the score. The steam jets can also be programmed for holidays and special occasions, even for every time a local sports team might score.

The size and scope of *Whistle Grove* make it an important urban icon for the city of Cincinnati, as the giant paddle wheel and steam clouds can be seen from across the river in Kentucky. Evoking the city's past life as a hub during the golden age of riverboats, *Whistle Grove* is a perfect example of Janney's public artworks: elegant, interactive, informative, and intriguing.

Rendering of *Whistle Grove*.

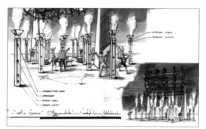

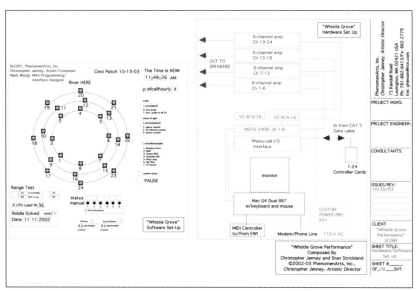

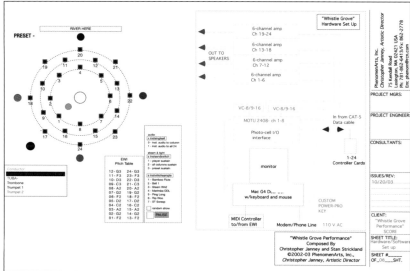

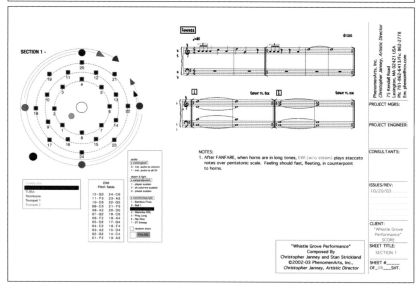

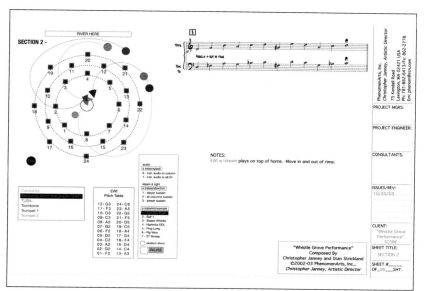

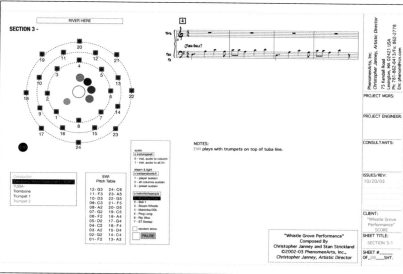

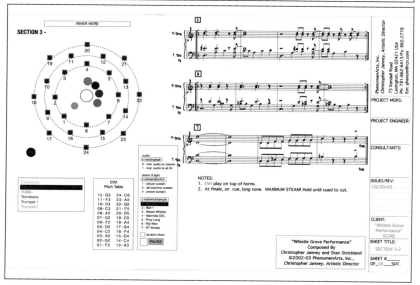

The musical score for *Whistle Grove* performance with Stan Strickland, 2002.

Pages 50-51: *Whistle Grove* in action.

Pages 52-53: *Whistle Grove* at night

Pages 54-55: *Whistle Grove*, framed by the Roebling Suspension Bridge and the Ohio River.

Turn Up the Heat
2000
American Airlines Arena
Miami, Florida

Janney had a slam dunk with his bold design for the scoreboard at the American Airlines Arena in Miami, Florida, home of the NBA's Miami Heat. In 1991, the executive vice president of the basketball franchise saw Janney's 1989 *Rainbow Pass*, created in conjunction with the Miami-based architectural firm Arquitectonica. She subsequently contacted Janney to design the season's opening ceremonies. In 1997, Arquitectonica was hired to design the new arena, and Janney was approached to create the scoreboard. In doing so, he brought a fresh approach to a standard arena element, sneaking a little art into the world of sports.

Having designed the season opener for two years, in 1991 and 1992, Janney understood the dynamics of "performing" for a captive audience of 18,000 screaming fans. A surround-sound system with Bose loudspeakers introduced the team in a spectacular way, enhanced by sounds such as jets flying overhead and birds in the Florida Everglades. Automated luminaires from Vari-Lite and multicolor lasers brought movement, color, and texture to the lighting.

Janney realized that, in spite of their interactive possibilities, scoreboards were pretty much a static item in the arena atmosphere. He visited stadiums in other cities to look at their scoreboards and decided that most were just big, boxy "visual boulders." His idea was to build a piece of performance sculpture that was visually lighter and more porous, one that would spring to life as part of the opening ceremonies for every home game. Titled *Turn Up the Heat*, the scoreboard was inaugurated on January 1, 2000, at the dawn of the new millennium.

Janney envisioned a design with far-reaching tentacles, resembling those of the anemone, an underwater creature he saw while scuba diving in South Florida. The long tentacles would reach out to grab and support the scoreboard. Once he had decided on the concept , Janney wondered who could build such a thing: a sculpture that would weigh 50,000 pounds but look as if it weighed just a tenth of that. He scoured the Internet and found Starnet International in Orlando, a company that built space frames for NASA and, therefore, understood how to make structures that were super-lightweight in relation to their size.

The engineers and aluminum experts at Starnet began to build the scoreboard: a sphere thirty feet in diameter, with ninety-six tentacles extending in all directions. The entire structure would be made of brushed aluminum; the tentacles would hold up the fourteen-by-nine-foot Mitsubishi electronic LED screens essential to the scoreboard. The content on the screens would be computer-generated—changeable with a keystroke.

Performance elements, including Vari-Lite automated luminaires, fog machines, strobe lights on the tips of the tentacles, and confetti cannons (used when the Heat won), would enhance the ambience of the games, bringing dynamic elements to an otherwise static object. Janney also composed a sound-score, using loudspeakers from the in-house system, to accompany the lighting effects during the opening ceremonies. "It is important for the fans to 'see the sound' when it is moving around the sphere," says Janney. "You can't hear that much when there are 18,000 people screaming."

Even in the late nineties, the idea of animation in architecture was relatively new. When Jay Cross, then the executive director of the Heat organization, quizzed Janney on what the scoreboard would actually "do" for the opening ceremonies, Janney prepared a computer-animated video, complete with music and simulations of fog, strobes, and indoor fireworks. When he saw it, Cross asked, "Can I have a copy? This will get us advertisers that are on the fence."

At the same time, Starnet generated a computer model based on Janney's drawings. Starnet's first attempt resembled an egg more than a sphere. "Here was a good example of what I learned by being an artist at MIT. Clearly, Starnet thought they had generated a form based on my design. But they had distorted the form enough to corrupt my vision of this spherical anemone. I had to slow them down and get them to see where they were veering offtrack. Remember, it is the artist's job to keep everyone focused on the clarity of the vision," says Janney, who did not want an oval or an ellipse. "The form is very important. In the end, it is the jewel in the center of this magnificent arena."

A green sea anemone.

To make sure that the second draft would indeed be round, Janney turned to a technique used by Renaissance architects: he made an exact, scaled, three-dimensional model of the work. He hung it in Starnet's computer lab so they could look at it from any angle and walk around it as they worked. The model helped. "You are looking at the real deal," Janney explains. "Computers can help us to visualize, but there is just no substitute for 3-D objects in the real world."

Janney designed the structure with two concentric geodesic spheres forming the structural core for the scoreboard, the inner sphere made of welded plates for additional stability. The outer sphere has struts that meet at hubs with concentric sleeves for supporting the four-inch rolled tubes that serve as tentacles. These are structurally connected to the inner and outer sphere and reach out to the LED video screens, stat boards, and ad boards.

Model of the geodesic sphere design for *Turn Up the Heat*.

Far from your everyday sports venue, this one redefines the concept of a basketball arena. The exterior has been likened to a furnace that glows red and yellow in concert with the sunset shimmering over Biscayne Bay. Arquitectonica designed a wraparound facade, punctuated by walls of glass that taper to an edge like the prow of an ocean liner. The exterior of the arena is a new architectural icon on the Miami cityscape, and Janney's scoreboard, suspended in the middle of the space, is its centerpiece: a work of iconoclastic performance art.

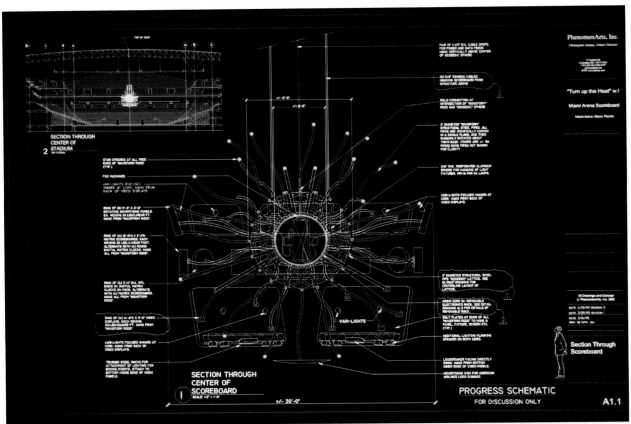

Opposite, top: Schematic drawing for *Turn Up the Heat*.
Opposite, bottom: *Turn Up the Heat* scoreboard on the floor for maintenance.
Top: Still image from computer animation of scoreboard.
Middle: Installation photo as scoreboard was assembled on site.
Bottom: Early presentation model of scoreboard design.
Overleaf: Sold-out crowd at American Airlines Miami Arena.

Harmonic Runway 1995
Miami International Airport
Miami, Florida

With his artwork, Janney seeks to encourage curiosity in harried travelers and imagination in jaded city dwellers. These public art projects include large-scale installations that take people by surprise in unexpected places, like airport terminals and parking structures. Janney not only adds art to these otherwise bland environments but also brings the architecture to life, turning buildings into urban icons that are destinations in themselves. One such example is *Harmonic Runway*, a site-specific, interactive installation that opened in 1995 at the Miami International Airport.

Janney won the commission to build this piece, beating out two other invited artists in a closed competition in 1991. Janney was already familiar with south Florida, having created *Rainbow Pass* in conjunction with the Miami-based architectural firm Arquitectonica, in 1989. He was also in tune with the flora and fauna of the area, thanks to his numerous scuba diving trips in the area.

Built into the parallel walls of a 180-foot passage with moving walkways running the length of the airport's Concourse A, *Harmonic Runway* is composed of 132 panes of colored glass, each ten feet in height. Divided into twelve bays, with eleven panels of glass per bay, the panes are laminated with Monsanto Opticolor film and are tilted at various angles to simulate a wave effect. During the day, sunlight passes through the glass, throwing bright color washes on passersby, while at night, Altman ZipStrips (long strips of light, with Ushio's 10,000-hour MR-16 lamps) and colored gels illuminate the glass panels. Twenty-four Martin Professional Roboscan automated luminaires add still another layer of moving forms and colors.

Janney had been experimenting with the effects of light on colored glass and resin for many years, long before the technology existed to execute a piece like *Harmonic Runway*. When he began to investigate his options for this competition, he discovered that Monsanto was about to launch a new range of 2,000 colors. Janney visited the company in western Massachusetts and considered the new product and *Harmonic Runway* to be a match made in heaven. He then enlisted associate Geoff Pingree to help him execute his vision.

When pedestrians walk past the structural columns, spaced twenty feet apart, Allen Bradley photoelectric cells stationed within these columns detect their motion. The sensors are spaced vertically as well as horizontally, so that people of various heights can trigger different patterns. When triggered, the sensors send information to Macintosh computers that shape the rhythm of Janney's melodic patterns in the space. The sensors also trigger composed sequences evocative of the tropical South Florida landscape, making the piece sound-specific as well as site-specific.

Moving through the zones of changing color, travelers can hear the chirping of crickets, the croaking of frogs, or the flapping wings of a flock of birds flying over the Everglades. The shapes and sounds of *Harmonic Runway* reveal the essence of South Florida through visual and aural stimuli, reinforcing Janney's philosophy of wanting people "to *experience* my pieces, not just see them." As people move through *Harmonic Runway* and realize that something is coming to life around them, many simply smile; others wave their arms to see what will happen.

Harmonic Runway is one of several projects where Janney successfully combined the harmonic, melodic, and rhythmic elements of music with architecture. The walkway's interactive environment of light, sound, and color allows Janney to control the harmonic and melodic aspects of music, while the rhythm is given over to the movement of people through a particular architectural space.

Janney's intent was to create a refreshing environment for the weary travelers passing through the Miami airport, which serves as the major gateway between the United States and Latin America. When he heard that locals had deemed the work "a triumphal arch for Miami" and "a new entryway to the city," Janney replied, "And that's to the city's credit—you don't get a second chance to make a first impression." Visually engaging, *Harmonic Runway* has appeared in films: Sidney Pollack's *Random Hearts*, starring Harrison Ford, and Joel Schumacher's *8mm*, starring Nicolas Cage. It was also used as the backdrop for a *Vogue* magazine fashion shoot and several music videos. Janney was the 1995 winner of General Electric's Edison Award, a prestigious prize in the lighting industry, for *Harmonic Runway*. Unfortunately, after the events of September 11, 2001, *Harmonic Runway* was dismantled, but Janney has hopes to recreate it elsewhere.

Janney refers to projects like *Harmonic Runway* as his "Urban Musical Instruments" and is interested in the interaction between people and buildings. "Can you have a physical relationship with a building?" he asks. "I like to push against the sense of alienation in the urban environment and add soul to faceless, nameless places. Lighting and sound are what bring life to a public space. These are two media beyond bricks and mortar that can break the barrier and reach out to people."

Still from computer animation for *Harmonic Runway*, 1991.

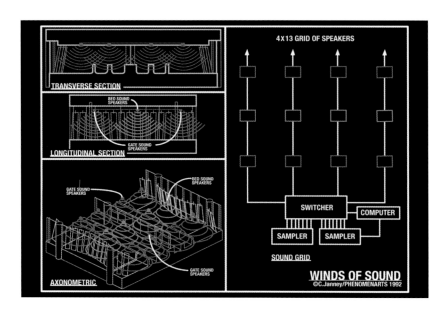

4X13 GRID OF SPEAKERS

SWITCHER | COMPUTER

SAMPLER | SAMPLER

SOUND GRID

WINDS OF SOUND
©C.Janney/PHENOMENARTS 1992

TRANSVERSE SECTION

BED SOUND SPEAKERS

GATE SOUND SPEAKERS

LONGITUDINAL SECTION

GATE SOUND SPEAKERS

BED SOUND SPEAKERS

GATE SOUND SPEAKERS

AXONOMETRIC

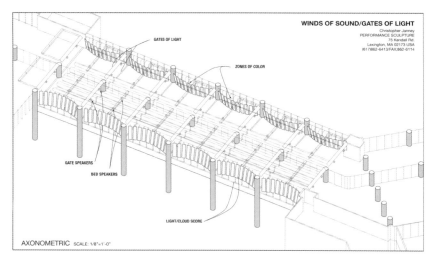

WINDS OF SOUND/GATES OF LIGHT
Christopher Janney
PERFORMANCE SCULPTURE
75 Kendall Rd.
Lexington, MA 02173 USA
(617)862-6413/FAX:862-6114

GATES OF LIGHT

ZONES OF COLOR

GATE SPEAKERS

BED SPEAKERS

LIGHT/CLOUD SCORE

AXONOMETRIC SCALE: 1/8"=1'-0"

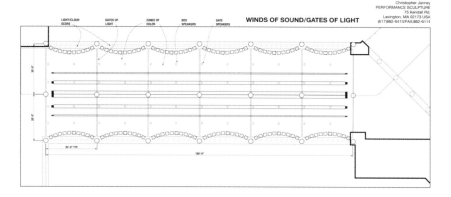

Christopher Janney
PERFORMANCE SCULPTURE
75 Kendall Rd.
Lexington, MA 02173 USA
(617)862-6413/FAX:862-6114

WINDS OF SOUND/GATES OF LIGHT

LIGHT/CLOUD SCORE | GATES OF LIGHT | ZONES OF COLOR | BED SPEAKERS | GATE SPEAKERS

Top: Schematic detail of light component.
Middle and bottom: Presentation drawings using working title, "Winds of Sound/Gates of Light," 1991.
Opposite, top: Full-scale studio mock-up.
Opposite, bottom: Detail of aluminum-glass connection.
Overleaf: *Harmonic Runway* in action.
Pages 68-69: Detail of single bay, *Harmonic Runway*.
Pages 70-71: *Harmonic Runway* seen from the exterior of the terminal.

Sonic Forest
1994–Present
Sonic Forest on Tour

Pittsburgh, PA, 1994; Lincoln Center, NYC, 1994
Bonnaroo Music & Arts Festival, Manchester, TN, 2005
Union Square, NYC, 2004
Sonic Forest "David's Way" (permanent installation), 2004
Sonic Forest on Tour '06: Various locations, US and UK

In 1991, Janney received a grant from the National Endowment for the Arts to develop an art project that could "plug into large, overscaled urban plazas, many of which are windswept civic wastelands with buildings set back too far from the street." The result was his 1995 project, *Sonic Forest*, a logical extension of his earlier work with *Soundstair*. The goal for the project was to bring a human scale back to the urban plaza and to make *Sonic Forest* a permanent element woven into the fabric of a city.

The concept for the NEA grant took seed in 1994, when Janney received a commission from the Three Rivers Festival in Pittsburgh, Pennsylvania. Following its debut in that city, *Sonic Forest* traveled to Philadelphia, Boston, and New York, where it appeared at Lincoln Center (Janney's 2002 piece, *Whistle Grove*, was a logical outgrowth of this investigation). The tour interested Janney, as the generic columns could be set up in different configurations as the work traveled from city to city.

Sonic Forest is composed of twenty-five eight-foot columns, each constructed of one-quarter-inch, dark blue aluminum tubing. The columns are outfitted with four photo-sensors so that four people can interact with each column at once. There are also lights and built-in loudspeakers, custom enclosures designed by Janney, using five-inch JBL drivers that fit neatly into the ten-inch-diameter columns. The columns themselves can be set up in a grid or a circle, to fit the physical requirements of each location, making *Sonic Forest* both a site-specific work and one that is flexible enough to be reinvented as needed.

When placed close together, the columns resemble electronic trees,

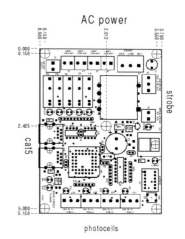

Schematic of printed circuit card for *Sonic Forest*.

making up a forest canopy. As people pass between the "trees," they explore the "sonic forest." The lighting system includes four small but bright MR-16 lamps that sit on top of the pillars. As people interact with the columns, the lamps shine as spotlights down on them. Spectators also trigger the sensors to produce continually changing patterns of preprogrammed sounds and spoken text, all accompanied by varying lighting effects.

When Janney turned on *Sonic Forest* for the first time, he not only found he had succeeded in building a "forest" on a human scale, but also realized he had a twenty-five-speaker surround-sound system. "I could program anything, from a flock of geese flying left to right overhead to a pack of barking dogs running through the installation." Janney then developed music expressly for the forest. "This is a good example of how the instrument revealed itself once it was built," he says.

In storage since 1995, *Sonic Forest* was taken out of mothballs in 2005 for the Bonnaroo Music and Arts Festival, a three-day music festival held on a 700-acre farm in Manchester, Tennessee. Ashley Capps, the festival producer, asked Janney, "What can you do for a crowd of 80,000 people?" Janney's answer was the revival of *Sonic Forest*, modified for a musical environment rather than an urban plaza.

At the Bonnaroo festival, *Sonic Forest* ran twenty-four hours a day as part of the continuous scene. The nonstop aspect excited Janney because the earlier versions of *Sonic Forest* were in locations that were active mostly during the day. As a night owl himself, Janney liked the fact that not only had *Sonic Forest* been reborn, but its reincarnation had placed it right in the middle of an around-the-clock music-appreciating environment. One change was the addition of a strobe-light beacon on the top of each column, timed to provide a rhythmic counterpoint to the other lighting elements.

The Bonnaroo *Sonic Forest* was installed on a 1,000-square-foot site. This time there were just sixteen columns, placed in four rows of four, twelve feet apart. Supplemental stacks of loudspeakers at the four corners of the installation enhanced the sonic environment. The technical systems were connected to a portable eight-by-eight-foot control booth that Janney called "the Sound House." He designed it with a roof deck for a "god's-eye view" of the forest and surrounding events.

A sixteen-column version of *Sonic Forest* with columns just four feet tall and made of burnished aluminum was installed in New York City's Union Square for a week in the spring of 2004. This installation was coproduced by Dancing in the Streets, Inc., as part of a citywide festival that Janney codirected, titled "New Sound, New York."

In 2005, *David's Way,* a permanent variation of *Sonic Forest,* was "planted" along a walking trail in downtown Dallas, Texas. It was a commission from the Meyerson family as a memorial for their son. Marlene Meyerson said she knew from the moment she saw Janney give a lecture in New York that he could create something that would embody the spirit and wit of her son, David. The piece has the interactive elements, but it also has "ghosts in the machine," which trigger fleeting light and sound patterns from time to time. This iteration is linear rather than square or round, with shorter, brushed-aluminum bollards. "They are more like electronic bushes than trees," says Janney. "The aluminum provides a nice counterpoint to nature."

Sonic Forest, Union Square, New York City, 2004.

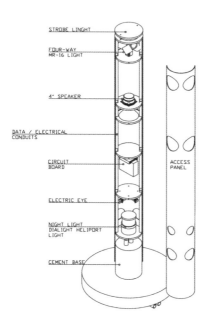

STROBE LINGHT

FOUR-WAY
MR-16 LIGHT

4" SPEAKER

DATA / ELECTRICAL
CONDUITS

CIRCUIT
BOARD

ELECTRIC EYE

NIGHT LIGHT
DIALIGHT HELIPORT
LIGHT

CEMENT BASE

ACCESS
PANEL

INTERACTIVE COLUMN AXONOMETRIC
SOUND FROREST   PHENOMENARTS, INC.   DRAWN BY JK

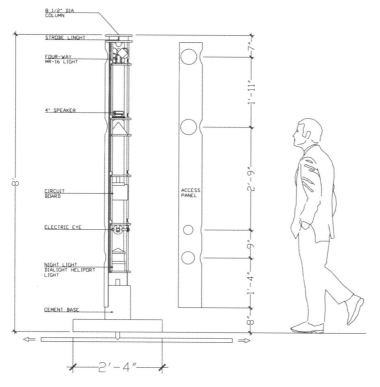

8 1/2" DIA
COLUMN

STROBE LINGHT

FOUR-WAY
MR-16 LIGHT

4" SPEAKER

CIRCUIT
BOARD

ELECTRIC EYE

NIGHT LIGHT
DIALIGHT HELIPORT
LIGHT

CEMENT BASE

ACCESS
PANEL

7"

1'-11"

2'-9"

9"

1'-4"

8"

8'

2'-4"

INTERACTIVE COLUMN SECTION
SOUND FROREST   PHENOMENARTS, INC.   DRAWN BY JK

This page, top and bottom: schematics of the "trees" in *Sonic Forest*.
Opposite, top: *Sonic Forest*, Lincoln Center, New York City, 1994.
Opposite, bottom: *Sonic Forest*, Union Square, New York City, 2004.
Overleaf: *Sonic Forest*, Bonnaroo Music and Arts Festival, Manchester, Tennessee, 2005.
Pages 78-79: *Sonic Forest*, Pittsburgh, Pennsylvania, 1994.

Circling
2005
South Concessions Area
Dallas–Fort Worth International Airport, Terminal D
Irving, TX

In his professional and personal life, Janney has spent quite a bit of time waiting in airports. Aware that this part of the travel experience was ripe for improvement, Janney decided to shake up the paradigm when he was commissioned for a major project for a new international terminal at Dallas–Fort Worth International Airport in Texas. His response was *Circling*, an interactive, three-dimensional labyrinth, the name of which reflects both the notion of planes circling overhead and the action of the passengers themselves as they circle through four concentric rings within the thirty-foot-diameter space.

As one of thirty international artists who created the impressive collection of artwork commissioned for International Terminal D (other artists and their works include Dennis Oppenheim's *Crystal Mountain,* Terry Allen's *Giant Wishbone,* and Anitra Blayton's sixteen-foot sculpture, *Standing Ovation*), Janney had a choice of sites. He selected a large concession area at the south end of the terminal, with its soaring sixty-five-foot ceilings, as the logical location for his installation.

Circling is based on a labyrinthine form but had to be configured for the airport space. Its walls, constructed from one hundred sheets of two-foot-wide colored glass, spiral at different heights, up to twelve feet, along terrazzo paths. Twenty-eight sensors embedded in the floor trigger lights and loudspeakers to reinforce the idea of illumination and sounds coming up from the earth as people walk through the maze. *Circling* is run by a high-speed G5 Macintosh computer, running PhenomenArts's MAX software, which was custom designed for this project. Twenty-eight amplifiers augment the sound system. All of the technical elements are located in an electrical room that sits fifty feet away from the maze, tucked into a space under an escalator.

Dubbed the "Blue Onion" by workers and frequent visitors to the airport, *Circling* has a decidedly blue glow, due to the blue, blue-green, and blue-violet tints in the glass panels. Janney refers to it as an "onion-like icon" that evokes the spiritual symbol of a circle: "It is more soothing to walk in a circle than in other shapes," he says. "Not that many people at the airport key into its spiritual side, but it provides a good way to escape from the hectic pace of the place."

Like Janney's *Touch My Building* (1998), the *Circling* environment has a riddle, etched in a plaque in the center of the piece, telling visitors which path to take to unlock the puzzle. (Janney can check in from his computer to see when and how many times it has been solved.) And like *Touch My Building*, one of Janney's goals for *Circling* was to reduce the scale of the building to a more human size and give it back to the people. As they approach it, travelers see *Circling* as a freestanding form. Upon closer examination, they realize that they can walk into it and interact with it.

When considering the options for *Circling*, an installation with a captive audience, Janney wondered what kind of work would best fit the space and capture the viewers' interest. "My thought was to create a game of some sorts—a soothing, quiet, contemplative game," he explains. "I then considered labyrinths and their historical significance; they are used for walking both for exercise and rest and have a calming, meditative effect."

The resulting concept was *Circling*, a twenty-first-century labyrinthine environment. It is, in effect, a game, using similar elements as those in Janney's other interactive sound/light environments. To give *Circling* a character of its own and to allow passengers to step out of the airport environment, Janney opted for walls of transparent, colored glass in concentric, maze-like circles. From the upper levels of the terminal, the concentric nature of the work is clearly seen, while at ground level, it appears to be what Janney calls "a series of veils."

Full-scale studio mockup of *Circling*.

As an artist, Janney is concerned that public spaces not only have a unique sense of place, but that they are also places of creative rest. He designs artworks that are both visually interesting and physically engaging enough to help spectators pass long hours of waiting. To that end, *Circling* attempts to make people aware of the scale and beauty of the grand space of Terminal D, while at the same time allowing them to develop a sense of belonging through imaginative play with interactive systems.

Circling is one of a number of artworks Janney designed for airports, as well as part of his Urban Musical Instrument series. It is also related to *Harmonic Runway*, Janney's earlier installation for the Miami International Airport. When it opened, *Circling* became Janney's largest piece in a major metropolitan airport. The technology may have changed in the intervening years, and the implementation of these projects may be smoother, but Janney's basic philosophy and fundamental concepts remain the same: His Urban Musical Instruments can be heard loud and clear.

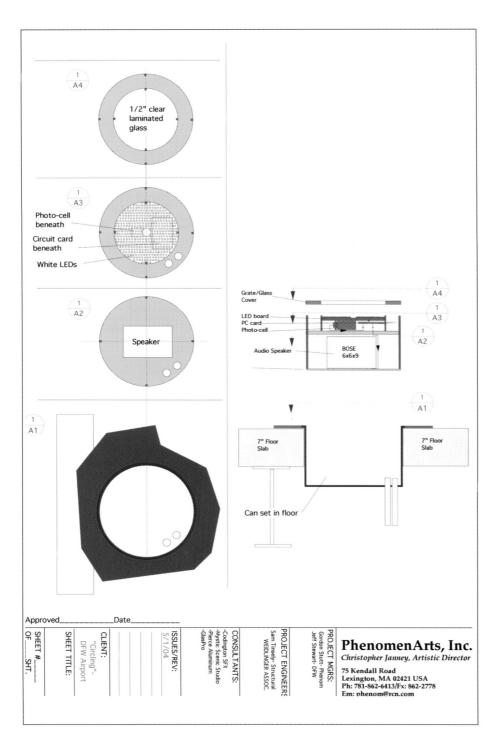

PhenomenArts, Inc.
Christopher Janney, Artistic Director

75 Kendall Road
Lexington, MA 02421 USA
Ph: 781-862-6413/Fx: 862-2778
Em: phenom@rcn.com

Left: Construction detail of interactive "floor cans"—the housing for speakers, lights, sensors, and electronics that animate *Circling*.
Top right: Interactive floor-can study denoting alternate light source.
Bottom right: Final design for floor/speaker grille.

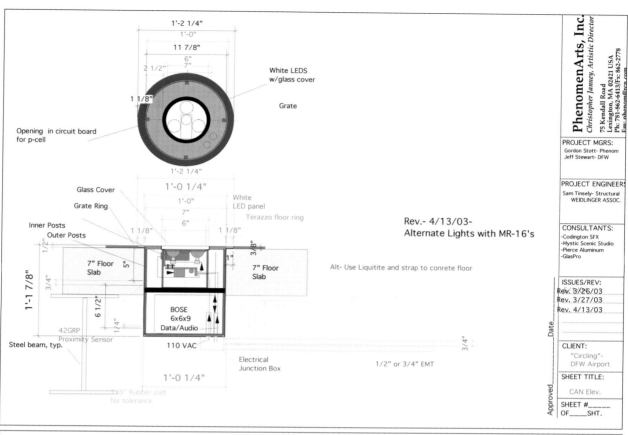

1'-2 1/4"
1'-0"
11 7/8"
6"
7"
2 1/2"
1 1/8"

White LEDS
w/glass cover

Grate

Opening in circuit board
for p-cell

1'-2 1/4"

1'-0 1/4"
1'-0"
7"
6"

Glass Cover
Grate Ring

Inner Posts
Outer Posts

White
LED panel
Terazzo floor ring

1 1/8"   1 1/8"

3/8"

1/2"

Rev.- 4/13/03-
Alternate Lights with MR-16's

7" Floor
Slab

5"

1"

7" Floor
Slab

Alt- Use Liquitite and strap to conrete floor

1'-1 7/8"

3/4"

6 1/2"

1/4"

BOSE
6x6x9
Data/Audio

42GRP
Proximity Sensor

Steel beam, typ.

110 VAC

Electrical
Junction Box

1'-0 1/4"

3/4"

1/2" or 3/4" EMT

1 1/8" Rubber pad
for tolerance

PhenomenArts, Inc.
Christopher Janney, Artistic Director
75 Kendall Road
Lexington, MA 02421 USA
Ph: 781-862-6413/Fx: 862-2778
Em: phenom@rcn.com

PROJECT MGRS:
Gordon Stott- Phenom
Jeff Stewart- DFW

PROJECT ENGINEERS
Sam Tinsely- Structural
WEIDLINGER ASSOC.

CONSULTANTS:
-Codington SFX
-Mystic Scenic Studio
-Pierce Aluminum
-GlasPro

ISSUES/REV:
Rev. 3/26/03
Rev. 3/27/03
Rev. 4/13/03

CLIENT:
"Circling"-
DFW Airport

SHEET TITLE:
CAN Elev.

SHEET #_____
OF_____SHT.

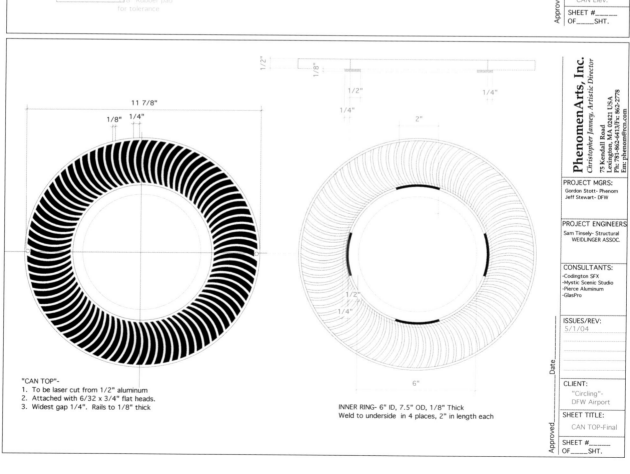

11 7/8"

1/8" 1/4"

1/2"

1/8"

1/2"

1/4"

1/4"

1/4"

2"

1/2"

1/4"

1/2"

1/4"

6"

"CAN TOP"-
1. To be laser cut from 1/2" aluminum
2. Attached with 6/32 x 3/4" flat heads.
3. Widest gap 1/4". Rails to 1/8" thick

INNER RING- 6" ID, 7.5" OD, 1/8" Thick
Weld to underside in 4 places, 2" in length each

PhenomenArts, Inc.
Christopher Janney, Artistic Director
75 Kendall Road
Lexington, MA 02421 USA
Ph: 781-862-6413/Fx: 862-2778
Em: phenom@rcn.com

PROJECT MGRS:
Gordon Stott- Phenom
Jeff Stewart- DFW

PROJECT ENGINEERS
Sam Tinsely- Structural
WEIDLINGER ASSOC.

CONSULTANTS:
-Codington SFX
-Mystic Scenic Studio
-Pierce Aluminum
-GlasPro

ISSUES/REV:
5/1/04

CLIENT:
"Circling"-
DFW Airport

SHEET TITLE:
CAN TOP-Final

SHEET #_____
OF_____SHT.

Presentation renderings for *Circling*.

Opposite top: Full-scale floor layout.
Opposite middle: Glass panel installation.
Opposite bottom: Detail of custom-built cart for glass installation.
This page: Final steps of installation.
Overleaf: *Circling*, completed project.

Physical
Music

HeartBeat
1983–Present

Fascinated by the pulsating rhythms of the human heart, Janney found a way to harness this sound and turn it into the primary layer of his musical score for *HeartBeat*, a performance piece that premiered in 1983, with the dancer Sara Rudner, of the Twyla Tharp Dance Company. The piece was recreated in 1998 as *HeartBeat:mb*, with the great Russian ballet dancer, Mikhail Baryshnikov, improvising solo movements to the sound of his own heart.

Janney started working on *HeartBeat* in 1981, as a research fellow at the MIT Center for Advanced Visual Studies (CAVS) in Cambridge, Massachusetts. His father's heart attack in 1979 and the invention of the first artificial heart in 1982 gave the artist food for thought about this vascular organ, as the central, mechanical pumping station of the human body, as well as the figurative seat of romance and the soul. As a drummer, Janney found the beat irresistible (considering it the "drumbeat of life") and turned to medical science and audio technology to find the equipment he would need to allow audiences to hear this life-sustaining sound onstage.

The medical equipment Janney employed to create *HeartBeat* includes a bioengineering device that monitors the electrical impulses from the brain to the heart and surrounding muscles. The device then sends these signals to a receiver via wireless telemetry, the science of automatic measurement and transmission of data from remote sources (also used to track wildlife, for example). In the case of *HeartBeat*, when the device is placed on the dancer's chest, it captures and amplifies these electrical pulses.

Through experimentation, Janney discovered that there is quite a bit of electrical "noise" in the body. As a result, he designed a set of custom audio filters so that the amplified sound heard in *HeartBeat* was indeed that of just the heart and its surrounding muscles. The heart throbs were layered with a musical score whose elements ranged from whispered jazz scat phrases to tabla (East Indian drums), with an additional layer of medical texts read by Janney himself. The score echoes the emotional as well as physiological functions of the heart, with the medical texts as a reminder of its scientific purpose.

In the original staged version of *HeartBeat*, Janney and Rudner choreographed movements based on a structure he devised. Janney was attracted to

Rudner's raw physicality and the multi-rhythmic nature of her movements, referring to them as "eurythmics on acid." Having worked with Twyla Tharp, who had been known for more than ten years for her fast-paced, loose-limbed, stylish modern dance, Rudner was no stranger to unusual assignments, and *HeartBeat* fit her like a glove. One dancer, three singers, Janney, and his machinery made up the cast. As Rudner danced, Janney discovered that the rhythm of the heart naturally speeds up or slows down as the dancer's speed changes, which meant that the singers had to follow the rhythm of Rudner's heartbeat to stay in sync.

In the mid-eighties, Baryshnikov asked Rudner to create a piece for his company, White Oak Dance Project. Rudner thought it would be interesting to bring Janney into the mix and to recreate *HeartBeat* with Baryshnikov. The result was *HeartBeat:mb* (the "mb" was added to differentiate this version from the first), which premiered in Paris during a European tour and then at New York's City Center in Manhattan as the first stop of a ten-city American solo tour featuring Mikhail Baryshnikov in *An Evening of Music and Dance*. Janney and Rudner worked with Baryshnikov on the shape and the choreographic direction of the piece, so that the actual movement became a structured improvisation. Due to Baryshnikov's extensive training in ballet and his Russian perspective, this piece had a much different quality than Rudner's original version.

The score was also different: Baryshnikov was touring with a string quartet and a concert pianist, so Janney decided to add new musical elements. Portions of the score were put into a sampler keyboard, which, as Janney explains, "looks like a piano but can create any sound you want. I recorded my voice reciting the various numbers and medical phrases." The pianist then played the keyboard in time to Baryshnikov's heartbeat. As the third section of the score, Janney had the string quartet play Samuel Barber's *Adagio for Strings*. A perfect choice for *HeartBeat:mb*, as Janney points out: "It's just for strings, with no percussion; the heartbeat and the strings coexist quite well."

"The pace of the thump-thump-thump both elicits his movement and reacts to it," wrote *Newsweek* about *HeartBeat:mb*. "Baryshnikov is practically translucent here: we see the still unsurpassed elegance of his classical technique, but we see it shaping moves that emanate directly from his personality, his very blood and breath."

The audience response to *HeartBeat:mb* was remarkable. People listened in silence as Baryshnikov's heart pumped faster, then slower, then seemed to soar as his arms flew through the air, and quieted to a static murmur when his head dipped below his chest, skipping a beat or two. At the end, some audience members were sobbing, perhaps thinking about loved ones whose hearts had stopped beating—a reminder of the fragility of human existence and the central role this organ plays in our physical body and creative imagination.

Over the twenty-five years since *HeartBeat* premiered, Janney has used the technology for many variations, not all of which have been onstage. In one version on a street corner, jazz saxophone player Stan Strickland performed over the beat of his own heart, with Janney and two singers providing the vocals. Janney has amplified his own heartbeat as an "underscore" to his lectures and even put the *HeartBeat* device on his one-year-old son during his christening, while Strickland accompanied the infant's heartbeat on flute.

Poster for sold-out performance of *Heartbeat:mb*, City Center, New York City, 1998.
Overleaf: Sara Rudner (left) and Stan Strickland (right) perform in *HeartBeat*.

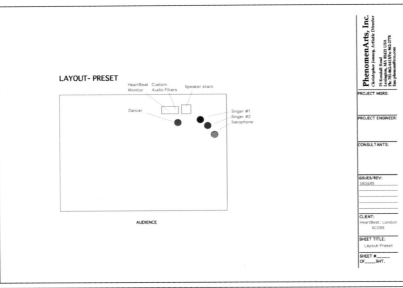

LAYOUT- PRESET

HeartBeat Custom
Monitor Audio Filters   Speaker stack

Dancer

Singer #1
Singer #2
Saxophone

AUDIENCE

PhenomenArts, Inc.
Christopher Janney, Artistic Director

75 Kendall Road
Lexington, MA 02421 USA
Ph: 781-862-4411Fx: 862-2778
Em: phenom@rcn.com

PROJECT MGRS:

PROJECT ENGINEER:

CONSULTANTS:

ISSUES/REV:
10/14/03

CLIENT:
HeartBeat: London
SCORE

SHEET TITLE:
Layout-Preset

SHEET #_____
OF_____SHT.

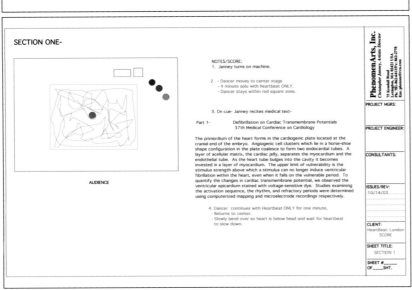

SECTION ONE-

AUDIENCE

NOTES/SCORE:
1. Janney turns on machine.

2. - Dancer moves to center stage
   - 4 minute solo with heartbeat ONLY.
   - Dancer stays within red square zone.

3. On cue- Janney recites medical text-

Part 1-   Defibrillation on Cardiac Transmembrane Potentials
               37th Medical Conference on Cardiology

The primordium of the heart forms in the cardiogenic plate located at the
cranial end of the embryo. Angiogenic cell clusters which lie in a horse-shoe
shape configuration in the plate coalesce to form two endocardial tubes. A
layer of acellular matrix, the cardiac jelly, separates the myocardium and the
endothelial tube. As the heart tube bulges into the cavity it becomes
invested in a layer of myocardium. The upper limit of vulnerability is the
stimulus strength above which a stimulus can no longer induce ventricular
fibrillation within the heart, even when it falls on the vulnerable period. To
quantify the changes in cardiac transmembrane potential, we observed the
ventricular epicardium stained with voltage-sensitive dye. Studies examining
the activation sequence, the rhythm, and refractory periods were determined
using computerized mapping and microelectrode recordings respectively.

4. Dancer continues with Heartbeat ONLY for one minute,
   - Returns to center.
   - Slowly bend over so heart is below head and wait for heartbeat
     to slow down.

PhenomenArts, Inc.
Christopher Janney, Artistic Director

75 Kendall Road
Lexington, MA 02421 USA
Ph: 781-862-4411Fx: 862-2778
Em: phenom@rcn.com

PROJECT MGRS:

PROJECT ENGINEER:

CONSULTANTS:

ISSUES/REV:
10/14/03

CLIENT:
HeartBeat: London
SCORE

SHEET TITLE:
SECTION 1

SHEET #_____
OF_____SHT.

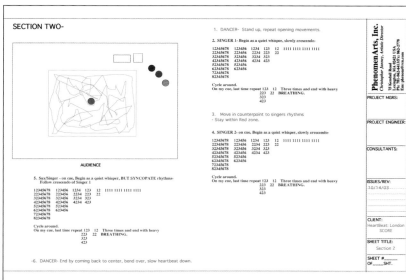

SECTION TWO-

AUDIENCE

1. DANCER- Stand up, repeat opening movements.

2. **SINGER 1-** Begin as a quiet whisper, slowly crescendo-

```
12345678   123456   1234   123   12   1111 1111 1111 1111
22345678   223456   2234   223   22
32345678   323456   3234   323
42345678   423456   4234   423
52345678   523456
62345678   623456
72345678
82345678
```

Cycle around.
On my cue, last time repeat   223   12   Three times and end with heavy
                              223   22   BREATHING.
                              323
                              423

3. Move in counterpoint to singers rhythms
- Stay within Red zone.

4. **SINGER 2-** on cue. Begin as a quiet whisper, slowly crescendo-

```
12345678   123456   1234   123   12   1111 1111 1111 1111
22345678   223456   2234   223   22
32345678   323456   3234   323
42345678   423456   4234   423
52345678   523456
62345678   623456
72345678
82345678
```

Cycle around.
On my cue, last time repeat   223   12   Three times and end with heavy
                              223   22   BREATHING.
                              323
                              423

5. Sax/Singer - on cue, Begin as a quiet whisper, BUT SYNCOPATE rhythms-
- Follow crescendo of Singer 1

```
12345678   123456   1234   123   12   1111 1111 1111 1111
22345678   223456   2234   223   22
32345678   323456   3234   323
42345678   423456   4234   423
52345678   523456
62345678   623456
72345678
82345678
```

Cycle around.
On my cue, last time repeat 123   12   Three times and end with heavy
                            223   22   BREATHING.
                            323
                            423

-6. DANCER- End by coming back to center, bend over, slow heartbeat down.

PhenomenArts, Inc.
Christopher Janney, Artistic Director
78 Kendall Road
Lexington, MA 02421 USA
Ph: 781-862-4445/Fax 862-2778
Em: phenon@tvca.com

PROJECT MGRS:

PROJECT ENGINEER:

CONSULTANTS:

ISSUES/REV:
10/14/03

CLIENT:
HeartBeat: London
SCORE

SHEET TITLE:
Section 2

SHEET #_____
OF_____SHT.

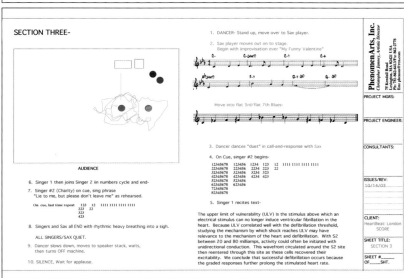

SECTION THREE-

AUDIENCE

1. DANCER- Stand up, move over to Sax player.

2. Sax player moves out on to stage.
Begin with improvisation over "My Funny Valentine"

Move into flat 3rd/flat 7th Blues-

3. Dancer dances "duet" in call-and-response with Sax

4. On Cue, singer #2 begins-

```
12345678   123456   1234   123   12   1111 1111 1111 1111
22345678   223456   2234   223   22
32345678   323456   3234   323
42345678   423456   4234   423
52345678   523456
62345678   623456
72345678
82345678
```

5. Singer 1 recites text-

6. Singer 1 then joins Singer 2 iin numbers cycle and end-

7. Singer #2 (Charity) on cue, sing phrase
"Lie to me, but please don't leave me" as rehearsed.

```
On  cue, last time repeat   123   12   1111 1111 1111 1111
                            223   22
                            323
                            423
```

8. Singers and Sax all END with rhythmic heavy breathing into a sigh.

ALL SINGERS/SAX QUIET.

9. Dancer slows down, moves to speaker stack, waits,
then turns OFF machine.

10. SILENCE, Wait for applause.

The upper limit of vulnerability (ULV) is the stimulus above which an
electrical stimulus can no longer induce ventricular fibrillation in the
heart. Because ULV correlated well with the defibrillation threshold,
studying the mechanism by which shock reaches ULV may have
relevance to the mechanism of the heart and defibrillation. With S2
between 20 and 80 milliamps, activity could often be initiated with
unidirectional conduction. This wavefront circulated around the S2 site
then reentered through this site as these cells recovered their
excitability. We conclude that successful defibrillation occurs because
the graded responses further prolong the stimulated heart rate.

PhenomenArts, Inc.
Christopher Janney, Artistic Director
78 Kendall Road
Lexington, MA 02421 USA
Ph: 781-862-4445/Fax 862-2778
Em: phenon@tvca.com

PROJECT MGRS:

PROJECT ENGINEER:

CONSULTANTS:

ISSUES/REV:
10/14/03

CLIENT:
HeartBeat: London
SCORE

SHEET TITLE:
SECTION 3

SHEET #_____
OF_____SHT.

Score for *HeartBeat*, illustrating multimedia
components.
Overleaf: Mikhail Baryshnikov in *HeartBeat:mb*.

Visual Music Project
2005–Present

Over the years, Janney has built various visual instruments—electronic keyboards or drums that allow his music to be seen in some form, from overhead screens, to steam jets, to cannons that fire. His ideas often exceeded the available technology that could tackle such concepts and translate them into a visually interesting performance or installation. Today, high-speed computer chips are fast enough to have caught up with Janney's imagination, allowing him to create and play with multiple images in real time, right along with other musicians onstage.

Since Janney was a college student in the heady, experimental days of the 1960s, he has been interested in developing lighting schemes that could serve as visual manifestations of his music. Every few years he would return to the concept. "If the technology could do this, then I could do that," he would muse. Now that the technology can, in fact, do some of the things he can dream up, he has been working with musicians who are members of the faculty at the Berklee College of Music in Boston to take his visualization theories to the next level.

Many people are familiar with musical screen savers, where the form of visual music is monophonic. Janney likens the experience to hearing just one string of a guitar. With high-speed computers, he can now play multiple images or patterns simultaneously on the screen, making the visual experience much richer and more complex, like using all six strings on a guitar for counterpoint harmony and chord patterns. With the synthesizer/keyboard, two high-speed Macintosh computers, two monitors, a Barco projector, a sixteen-by-twelve-foot screen, and any mix of other performers, Janney is ready to jam. The audience sees the visual images from Janney's mix of his own synthesizer/keyboard and elements he selects from other musical instruments onstage.

Janney continually updates his "instrument" to include the fastest Macintosh computers available at the moment, in order to "play" images in real time. Using two computers, he incorporates both analog and digital images into the visual landscape. For a performance titled *Beyond Visible Light*, Janney projected a series of ultraviolet images ranging from X-rays of human and animal skulls, to deep space in the galaxy, to the stress diagram of a building (another intersection of his music and architecture). To increase the visual excitement, Janney's unique instrument can mix any combination of multiple images, resulting in intriguing, thought-provoking collages on the big screen.

The images can also change color subtly, almost in slow motion. While these analog images are pulled from the computer's memory, the digital component adds images and forms that Janney "plays" within the rhythmic forms of the music. For one of Janney's compositions, titled *Stop Time in Deep Space*, the bass and keyboards play in a 12/8 tempo, while the trumpet and saxophone play a syncopated melody line in straight 4/4 on top. Janney then projects images in counterpoint to these meters, attempting to make a visual rhythm on top of the music. This experience, where certain rhythmic information comes in through the ears and other information comes in through the eyes, is Janney's attempt at establishing "synaesthetic" music.

On occasion, to make the images as large as possible, Janney replaces the screen with a cyclorama, a theatrical drape that covers the entire backstage wall. Always interested in the newest technology, he has experimented with the latest developments in projection equipment, such as LED screens and multiple plasma screen systems. He has also experimented with taking the screen off the stage and into the performance environment, creating an interactive environment with a DJ and live musicians in a dance club.

What initially gave Janney the idea that music was visual? As a child, he was as fascinated with the fingers moving on a piano as listening to the performance. In the sixties, he built sound-sensitive light boxes. But now, Janney says, "My life is no longer about *why*. At 55, I don't question the ideas that come to me. At this point, I have to trust my intuition and watch where it wants to take me." Janney pursues his ideas with passion, not allowing his conscious mind to step in and tell him that any of his ideas are "worthless, dumb, or already-been-done." Janney cites the acclaimed Disney film *Fantasia* as an early example of animated explorations of classical music, but its technology was limited to what was available in 1940, when Walt Disney was pursuing his vision. The twist that makes the twenty-first-century brand of visual music interesting for Janney is being able to do it in real time.

Jamming with Moksha, a Berklee faculty band that performs four songs in a continuous, ninety-minute set, Janney has taken his visual music project to a new level. As for the audience, "They want more," he says. "The time flies by. This is a very immersive experience—in music and visual information."

Examples of Janney's projected images.

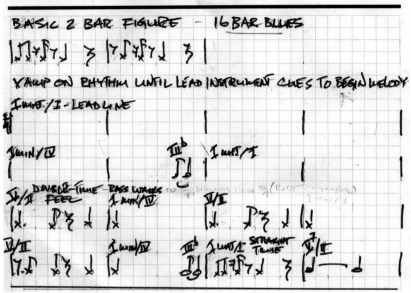

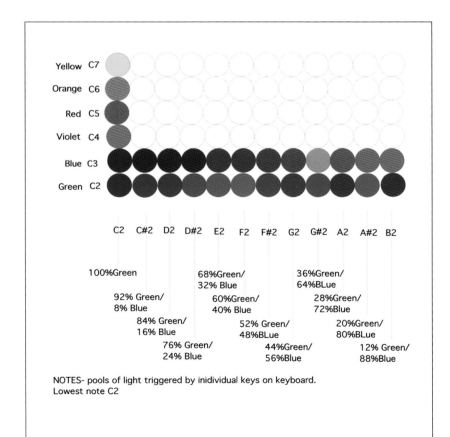

NOTES- pools of light triggered by inidividual keys on keyboard.
Lowest note C2

Top: Sketch for music score, *Stop Time in Deep Space*.
Bottom: Example of color pattern for color synthesizer.

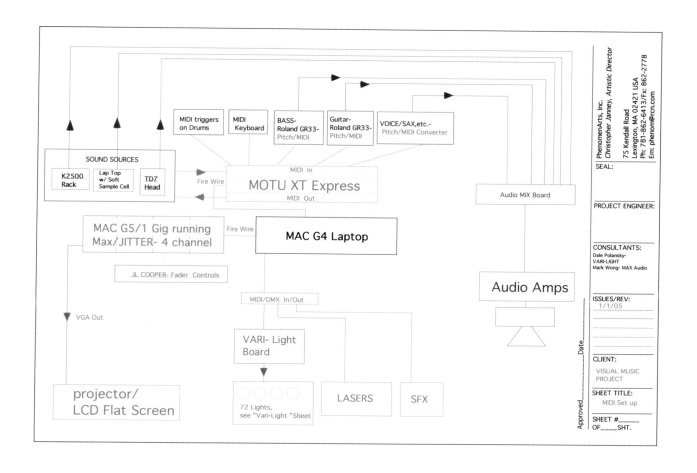

PhenomenArts, Inc.
Christopher Janney, Artistic Director

75 Kendall Road
Lexington, MA 02421 USA
Ph: 781-862-6413/Fx: 862-2778
Em: phenom@rcn.com

SEAL:

PROJECT ENGINEER:

CONSULTANTS:
Dale Polansky-
VARI-LIGHT
Mark Wong- MAX Audio

ISSUES/REV:
1/1/05

Date

CLIENT:
VISUAL MUSIC
PROJECT

SHEET TITLE:
MIDI Set up

SHEET #_____
OF_____SHT.

Approved

MIDI triggers on Drums

MIDI Keyboard

BASS-
Roland GR33-
Pitch/MIDI

Guitar-
Roland GR33-
Pitch/MIDI

VOICE/SAX,etc.-
Pitch/MIDI Converter

SOUND SOURCES

K2500 Rack

Lap Top w/ Soft Sample Cell

TD7 Head

Fire Wire

MIDI In
MOTU XT Express
MIDI Out

Audio MIX Board

MAC G5/1 Gig running Max/JITTER- 4 channel

Fire Wire

MAC G4 Laptop

Audio Amps

JL COOPER- Fader Controls

VGA Out

MIDI/DMX In/Out

VARI- Light Board

projector/
LCD Flat Screen

72 Lights, see "Vari-Light "Sheet

LASERS

SFX

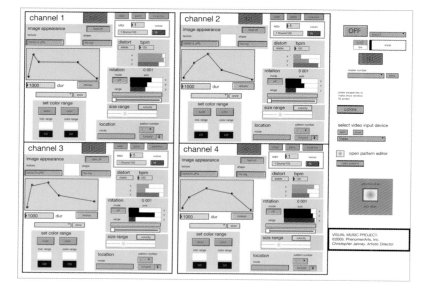

Top: Schematic layout of hardware components.
Bottom: Software interface.
Overleaf, left, top and bottom: Conceptual drawings of stage setups.
Overleaf, top right: Performance images with Moksha at Berklee Performance Center, Boston, 2005.
Overleaf, bottom right: Performance at Avalon Dance Club, Boston, with Stan Strickland, Wes Wirth, and DJ Wilke.

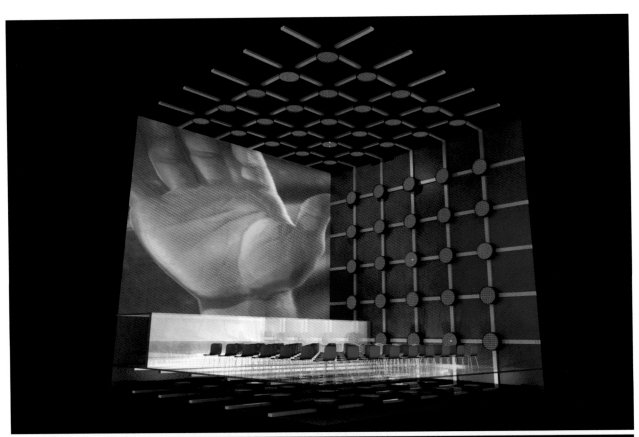

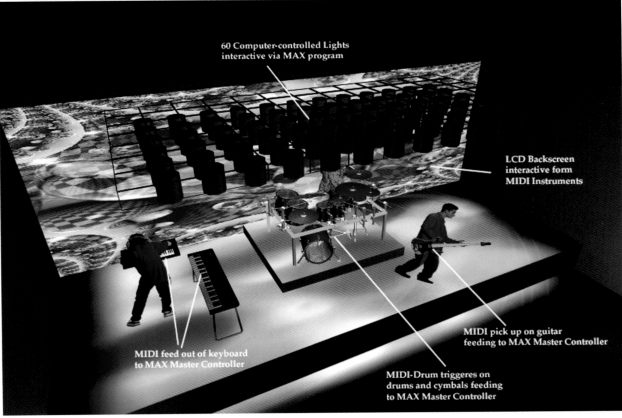

60 Computer-controlled Lights
interactive via MAX program

LCD Backscreen
interactive form
MIDI Instruments

MIDI pick up on guitar
feeding to MAX Master Controller

MIDI feed out of keyboard
to MAX Master Controller

MIDI-Drum triggeres on
drums and cymbals feeding
to MAX Master Controller

Performance
Architecture

A House Is a Musical Instrument: Kona
2000
Private residence
Big Island, Hawaii

The Kona coast, on the Big Island of Hawaii, is the site for one of Janney's unique architectural projects: an 8,000-square-foot private residence completed in 2000, after a three-year design/build process. A harmonious blend of natural materials, incorporating glass, wood, water, and lava stone, this home is part of his *A House Is a Musical Instrument* series.

Janney was originally hired by John Ryan, the owner of the Kona house, to consult on a design approach for Ryan's "Bank of the Future" project in Stamford, Connecticut. When Ryan approached Janney about designing his home in Hawaii, Janney was at first a bit surprised. (He told Ryan, "If you're serious, call me in the morning after the alcohol has worn off.") Janney soon became extremely excited about the prospect of exchanging ideas with Ryan and the possibility of developing some long-standing architectural concepts together with him. The result is a one-of-a-kind dream house, nestled on a triangular piece of land, facing west toward the Pacific Ocean, that has been featured in *Architectural Digest* and on HGTV's *Extreme Homes* program.

The house took one year to design and two years to build. Janney initially flew to Hawaii to survey the site and discuss plans for the house with Ryan. The two then met again in Hawaii for a few days, at which point the initial parameters for the house began to take shape, with its basic intent grounded in the principles of modernist philosophy: a series of freestanding, geometric planes holding up the cedar-shingled hip roof—a necessity to conform with local design codes. The house sits on terra firma but has a rooftop observation deck outfitted with a high-powered telescope to "fly up into the sky," as Janney puts it, and, below grade, a wine cellar to "burrow down into the earth."

Studio set-up during design period of *A House Is a Musical Instrument: Kona.*

All corners of the house are made of a colored glass, which throws tinted shadows that change shape and hue throughout the day as the sun peeks through. A skylight, also constructed of colored glass cut into triangular panels, serves as a giant environmental sundial, with a circular white oculus in the center.

One of the more unusual rooms is the underground wine cellar. In keeping with the topographical history of Hawaii, Janney designed this room to resemble a lava tube—a tunnel that is burned into the earth as hot lava pours out of a volcano. Some of the building materials also echo the local landscape, including Koa, a beautiful hardwood native to the island, as well as cut lava-stone slices set in geometric patterns in the exterior walls.

Working with a local interior design firm, Philpotts and Associates, Janney decided that each room in the house would be based on the variation of a single color, from red and blue for the two guest rooms to green for the master bedroom. Natural materials in these colors were chosen when possible—for example, a pearly blue marble in a guest bathroom and a deep, emerald green marble in the master bath.

An interior garden in the center of the house adds a note of serenity and brings a water element into the design. A small, 8,000-gallon pond, fed from a well cored ninety feet deep into ocean water, serves as a sanctuary for a sampling of fish from the South Seas (but no sharks, as Janney points out). The water theme is evident even upon entering the house, where a trough and water misters lead to the pond. As one walks down into the wine cellar, it is possible to look back into the pond through a glass wall. Here, the water element is restated from a different view, much like the recapitulation of a theme in a musical composition.

Conceptual rendering for the master bedroom.

In fact, music is another motif in the house, centered around a Steinway Model B mahogany grand piano with a sixteenth-century drawing by Robert Fludd (based on the Pythagorean theorem and the relationship of music to the planets) laser-etched into its top. For Janney, the piano is the heart of the house and reflects the yin and yang of his explorations in music and design. As the house is not Ryan's primary residence, Janney installed a MIDI-based system so that the piano plays itself a few minutes each day—at sunrise, noon, sunset, and midnight—to keep the instrument's components from drying out. The system calls the U.S. Naval Observatory on the Internet to get the exact time the sun will rise and set over Hawaii each day.

Echoing this sunrise/sunset theme is Janney's *Sun-Moon Clock,* set in the floor of the main living room. A digital readout tells the time for sunrise and sunset, moonrise and moonset, each day. The clock is strategically placed in the living room, at the exact point where one of the structural columns was cut out over a twenty-foot span to allow for a clearer view of the ocean, 300 feet in front of the house. Steel in the roof compensates for the missing column, but, thematically, Janney wanted the clock here to represent the idea that the column exists metaphorically. This notion of "sun/moon time" is a fundamental foundation of the temporal/musical concepts within the house.

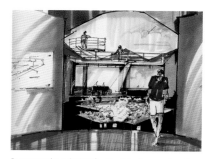

Conceptual rendering for the interior courtyard.

For Janney, the house was a once-in-a-lifetime opportunity, an architect's dream. "How often do you get a client who says, 'Design the dream house'?" he muses. "John and I are good friends, and we developed these ideas together. What I like best about this house is the opportunity that I had to realize some architectural concepts I have developed for over thirty years."

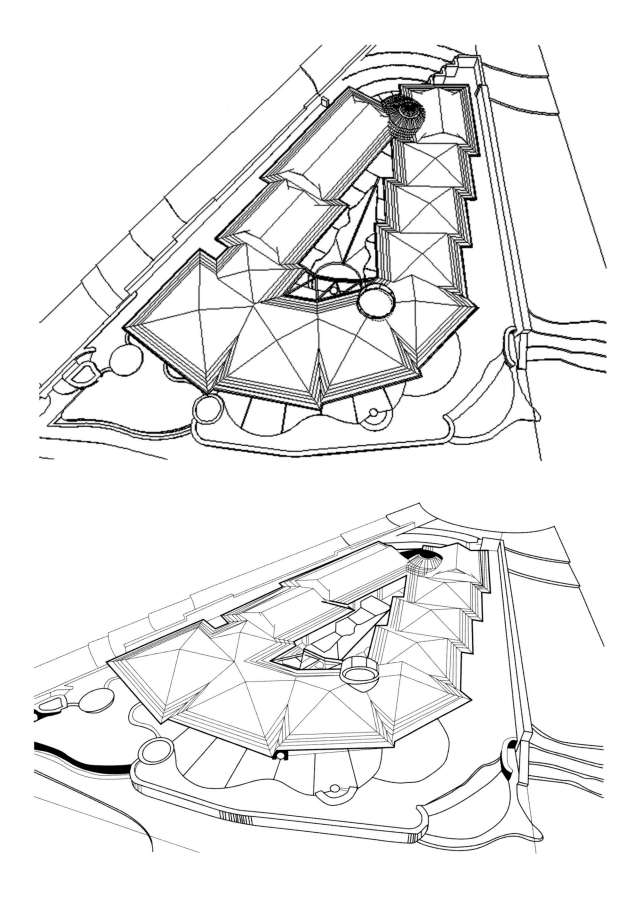

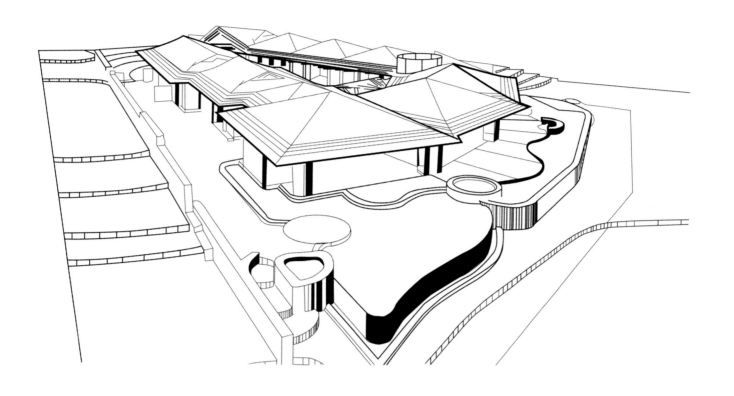

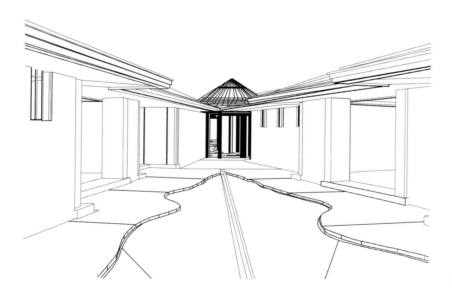

Computer renderings for various views of
Kona House, 1999.

Kona House under construction.

Page 114, top left: View of lower living room with stair to observation deck.

Page 114, top right: Master bedroom.

Page 114, bottom: Underground wine cellar with fish sanctuary.

Page 115: View of outdoor dining room overlooking pool.

Page 116: Moon gate.

Page 117: Colored shadow pattern from overhead skylight; circles denote equinox and solstice.

Page 118, top: *Sun-Moon Clock.*

Page 118, bottom: Custom-designed dining room table and chairs.

Page 119: Laser-cut inlay in baby grand piano features Robert Fludd's depiction of the Pythagorean monochord: *The Music of the Spheres.*

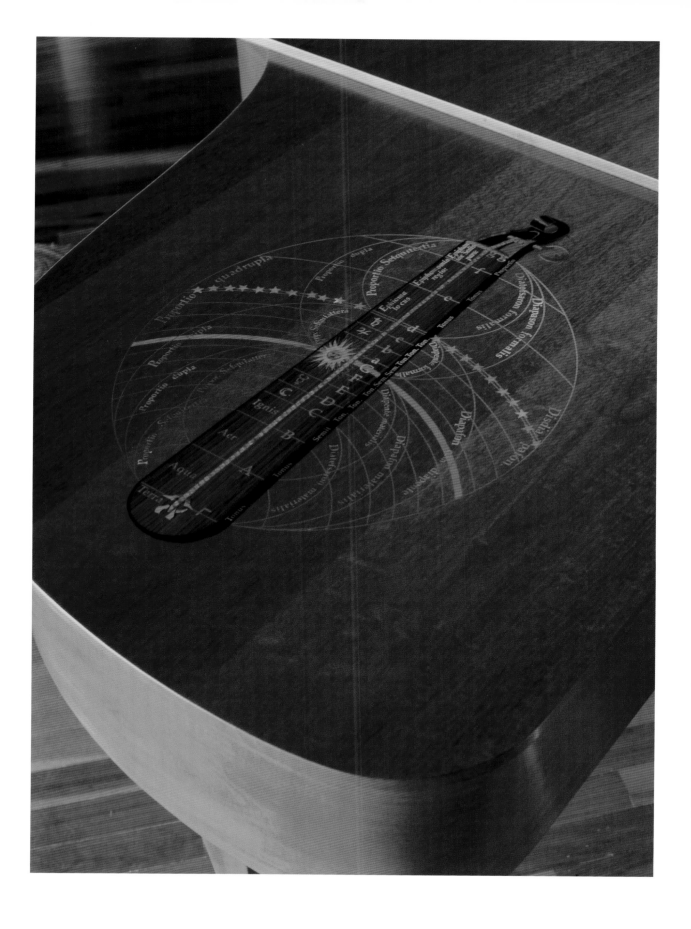

A House Is a Musical Instrument: Lexington
2004
Private residence
Lexington, Massachusetts

The house at 75 Kendall Road in Lexington, Massachusetts, is where Janney lives with his wife, two teenage children, an Australian Shepherd, and two cats. It is also the home base for his design firm and music studio, PhenomenArts, Inc. Titled *A House Is a Musical Instrument: Lexington*, it is one of a series of architectural projects that explore the nexus of architecture and music. Janney observes, "Le Corbusier said, 'A house is a machine for living.' I say a house is a musical instrument to be played."

The artist's most recent "musical instrument" started out as a 1929 New England farmhouse located approximately fifteen miles from Boston. The facade that fronts the street has been left intact, but as one passes by, unusual forms peek out from one side of the off-white structure. These modernist additions create a counterpoint to the conservative house, allowing the old and the new to cohabitate. Their juxtaposition provides visual interest that increases as one moves around to the back of the house, where there is a deck with a Coleman spa and an outdoor fireplace.

The Janney residence has been referred to as a "ship's deck" or a "little Guggenheim," but it stands to reason that the raw energy and creative artistry that Janney pours into his art projects would seep into his personal world, as well. However, 75 Kendall Road is more than just an objet d'art. It also meets the demanding requirements of an active family.

Janney and his wife like to have their kids socialize at home, so one of his priorities was to provide a cool space where his kids would feel excited to hang out with friends: the house comes equipped with a large gathering space (the "big room"—enough room for forty to fifty people—and a big-screen TV

A scale model of the Lexington house.

(the perfect spot for their annual Super Bowl party). Janney likes to keep the kids where he and his wife can "discreetly observe."

Another—literally—cool feature of the house is the underground recording studio, complete with isolation booth. Here Janney jams and lays down tracks (as does his son, who is also a musician). Access to the recording studio is gained through a circular staircase enveloped in an inverted, conical tower of rose-colored glass. A challenge to build, the hyperbolic sections of glass were rendered on Janney's computer, built in wood laminates for a sample fitting, then sent to a glass fabricator.

Janney built the additions onto the house himself, with the help of two carpenters. The challenge was to test the limits of what he could design and what they could actually build. The form of the new echoes the old, and then takes off in new directions. For example, a Palladio-style curved wall on the east side, facing the street, becomes a more radical, dark blue, conical section leaning out and "breaking away" from the building on the west side—Janney calls it the "fall-out wall." Janney couldn't find any local carpenters who knew how to build that kind of conical shape, so, drawing on dressmaking techniques, he sat up on the scaffolding himself, cutting large sheets of cardboard and fitting them onto the curved frame of two-by-sixes. Then the carpenters simply traced the cardboard shapes, cut them out of plywood, and Janney nailed them to the frame. Janney enjoyed this kind of architectural improvisation, another instance of bringing a musical experience into architecture. This final form became the dominant shape for the rear of the house, accentuated by its deep, royal blue color.

This house has one of two *Sun-Moon Clock*s that Janney has designed (the other is in *Kona House*, in Hawaii). In his own house, Janney placed the clock in the two-story entry foyer, on a wall on the second floor. Above the clock is a skylight made up of two ellipses of rose-colored glass. Their orientation allows one to cast a perfect circle of light when the sun is at its zenith on the winter solstice (12:36 p.m. in Lexington), while the other does the same on the summer solstice. Janney sees the clock and ellipses as a site-specific "meditation on sidereal time, an awareness of the rhythms of the earth, moon, and sun, and their recurring relationships to one another."

The front door to the house is an homage to Leonardo da Vinci's drawing *Man is the Measure of All Things*, which depicts a man standing within a circle and a square. Here, the door serves as an introduction to the overall experience offered by the house, and its design features a rectangle, of perfect golden-section proportions, framed within a circle. Other features include panels of colored glass located throughout the house, which allow colored light and shadows to paint the rooms with different hues during the day: the colors of the walls change as the sunlight changes. As Janney points out, "Traditionally, painting and sculpture are considered atemporal art forms; they are objects to look at. On the other hand, music is a temporal art form. You cannot look at it; it passes by you over time. But architecture is unique—it can possess both." By building a temporal house for himself and his family, Janney can move through his home and observe the colors changing every day and each year, bringing these and other temporal surprises of his music into the sphere of his architecture.

Construction photo, 2002.

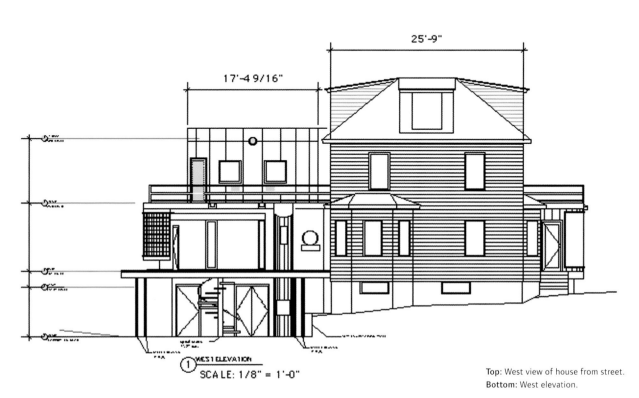

17'-4 9/16"

25'-9"

① WEST ELEVATION
SCALE: 1/8" = 1'-0"

Top: West view of house from street.
Bottom: West elevation.

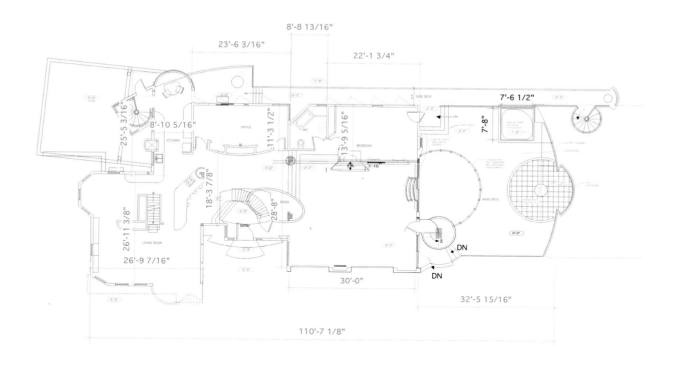

8'-8 13/16"

23'-6 3/16"

22'-1 3/4"

7'-6 1/2"

7'-8"

25'-5 3/16"

8'-10 5/16"

11'-3 1/2"

13'-9 5/16"

18'-3 7/8"

28'-8"

26'-11 3/8"

26'-9 7/16"

30'-0"

32'-5 15/16"

110'-7 1/8"

DN

DN

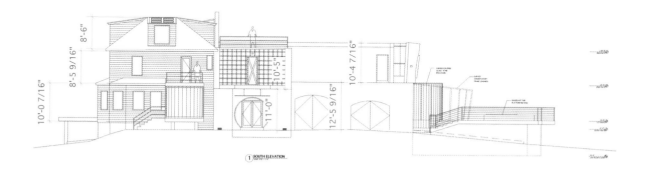

8'-6"

8'-5 9/16"

10'-0 7/16"

10'-5"

11'-0"

12'-5 9/16"

10'-4 7/16"

① SOUTH ELEVATION

Top: Plan for Lexington house.
Bottom: South elevation.
Overleaf: East elevation with rose-colored glass stair tower and blue fallout wall.

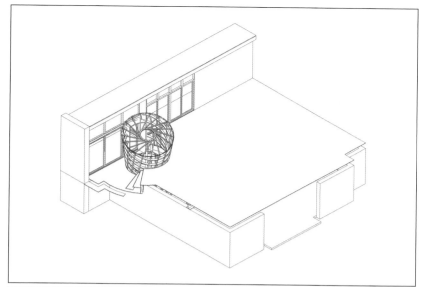

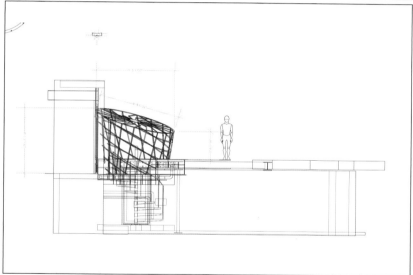

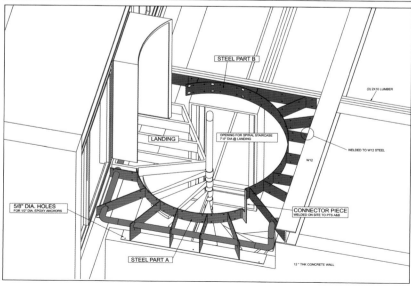

STEEL PART B

(3) 2X10 LUMBER

WELDED TO W12 STEEL

LANDING

OPENING FOR SPIRAL STAIRCASE
7'-0" DIA @ LANDING

W12

5/8" DIA. HOLES
FOR 1/2" DIA. EPOXY ANCHORS

CONNECTOR PIECE
WELDED ON SITE TO PTS A&B

STEEL PART A

12" THK CONCRETE WALL

Opposite: Detail of rose-colored stairway.
Left and above: Drawings and construction photos of rose-colored stairway.
Overleaf left: Interior of entry hall and staircase.
Overleaf right: Interior shot of rose-colored stair tower.

Opposite: Two views of "the big room."
This page, top left: Blue fall-out wall.
Bottom left: Daughter Lilli's bedroom.
Top and bottom, at right: Construction photos
of frame for circular window.

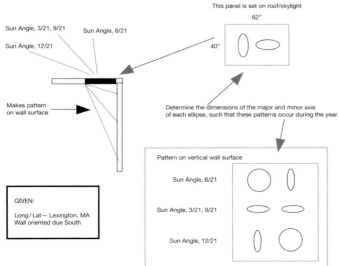

This panel is set on roof/skylight

62"

40"

Sun Angle, 3/21, 9/21   Sun Angle, 6/21

Sun Angle, 12/21

Makes pattern
on wall surface

Determine the dimensions of the major and minor axis
of each ellipse, such that these patterns occur during the year.

Pattern on vertical wall surface

Sun Angle, 6/21

Sun Angle, 3/21, 9/21

Sun Angle, 12/21

GIVEN:

Long / Lat— Lexington, MA
Wall oriented due South

Top: *Sun-Moon Clock*.
Bottom: Drawing for elliptical cutouts in roof
Opposite: *Sun-Moon Clock* in the Lexington
house, with elliptical projections from the roof
cutouts.

Resonating Frequencies 2004–Present

For more than a decade, Janney has taught a popular course at both the Irwin S. Chanin School of Architecture of the Cooper Union and the Pratt Institute in New York City. The course, titled "Sound as a Visual Medium," encourages students to think about the relationship between architecture and music, his two chief disciplines. Desiring to take his reflections to a new level, Janney contacted his old friend and colleague, Elise Bernhardt, who was at that time the executive director of The Kitchen, an alternative performance space in downtown Manhattan. Many famous musicians, including Laurie Anderson, Philip Glass, and Steve Reich, are alumni of the center, and Janney proposed that it co-sponsor a festival bringing together musicians and architects.

Janney's timing was fortuitous. The spring of 2004 marked the twenty-fifth anniversary of New Music America, a seminal contemporary music festival. To celebrate, a month-long event named "New Sound, New York" was planned, including an installation of Janney's signature Urban Musical Instrument *Sonic Forest*, in Manhattan's Union Square Park. Janney also curated four evening events under the title "Resonating Frequencies," dialogues in which leading architects and musicians shared their thoughts with him.

Organized in conjunction with the Kitchen and Cooper Union, these dialogues on architecture and music were thought provoking. The four pairs of interlocutors were the concept artist/musician/writer DJ Spooky and architect/architectural theorist Greg Lynn; minimalist composer Philip Glass and architect Thom Mayne; performance artist/composer Laurie Anderson and landscape architect Martha Schwartz; and electronic musician Moby and architect/educator Bernard Tschumi. These may appear to be odd couples who don't share much mutual terrain; in fact, DJ Spooky and Greg Lynn had worked together on a conceptual project, and the others quickly found common ground as they explored contemporary issues in their respective fields.

"Resonating Frequencies" explored interesting ideas, from Greg Lynn's idea of transformable buildings to DJ Spooky's story about Buddhist monks who burned down a shrine and then chanted as they recalled the architecture and

Postage stamp created by Janney for *Resonating Frequencies*.

used the memory to build a new shrine. Philip Glass noted, "Architecture is what you stumble over in the dark. You don't stumble across music in the dark." Thom Mayne "wanted to make architecture that hurt." Laurie Anderson referred to "what it's like to use your ears in the complex ocean of sound we live in." Martha Schwartz noted that sound is everywhere: "It's a spatial thing—people are claiming space using sound." Moby commented that "music is meant to be out in the world, getting dirty," to which Bernard Tschumi replied that this was "a perfect definition of architecture: architecture is never pure."

Through discussions with the various pairs of artists, Janney gave each lecture a theme or launching pad. DJ Spooky and Greg Lynn began with the proposition that "if architecture is frozen music, does that mean music is liquid architecture?" He framed Laurie Anderson and Martha Schwartz "in a Zen garden with Mozart and James Brown." Philip Glass and Thom Mayne (winner of the 2005 Pritzker Prize) pondered the relevance of "the Pythagorean theorem and the music of the spheres in the twenty-first century." Moby and Bernard Tschumi expounded on the idea of "music and architecture getting dirty," or corrupted, once it is out in the real world.

The emphasis of the evenings was not only on the discussions but also on twenty-minute performances by the musicians, including DJ Spooky with his turntables, demonstrating scratching techniques as he mixed his own brand of music and culture. Philip Glass brought a section of a film for which he had recently scored music. The architects added visual elements as well, showing images and animations of what they considered relevant "musical" projects.

Were any conclusions drawn from the four dialogues? "We weren't looking for conclusions as much as looking for new questions, new ways to think about the two different disciplines," admits Janney, who notes that as early as 4000 BC, the Egyptian pyramids were an example of the divine relationship between design and music. "This relationship may be less obvious today, embedded and expressed in different cultures," he adds. "The new paradigm, or Zeitgeist, of architecture, music, contemporary technology, and consciousness is an interesting intersection, generating new directions. Although, as it turned out, the Pythagorean theories and golden proportions of the planets weren't so divine after all, I think we are finding other, deeper expressions of architecture and music. We are seeing relationships not just of proportion, but of the soul and spirit of each discipline mixing into the other. As the Swallows used to sing, 'It ain't the meat, it's the motion.'"

Janney with architect Bernard Tschumi and musician/producer Moby.

Janney is planning a second round of dialogues. The players include the architect and concert pianist Raphael Viñoly together with Janney, who will be playing his visual synthesizer in the Jazz at Lincoln Center complex, which was designed by Viñoly; Daniel Libeskind, the architect of the winning entry in the competition to rebuild Ground Zero (he says his favorite architect is Johann Sebastian Bach), who will collaborate with musician/artist David Byrne; Liz Diller, the first architect to receive a MacArthur "genius" grant (with her partner, Richard Scofidio), and Walter Becker, the musician and cofounder of the band Steely Dan. Although Janney is not alone in his thinking about the relationship of architecture and music, he may be the foremost practitioner and promoter of their synthesis in real world applications.

Janney with landscape architect Martha Schwartz and musician Laurie Anderson.

Sonic Reflections

by Christopher Janney

with Carol Bankerd & Amy Bernhardt

OBVIOUS

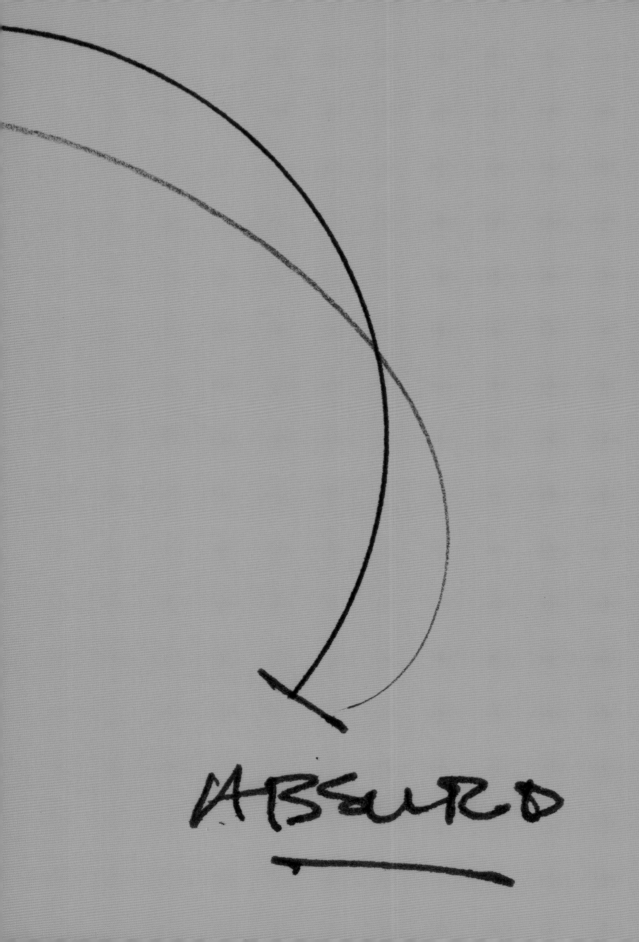

ABSURD

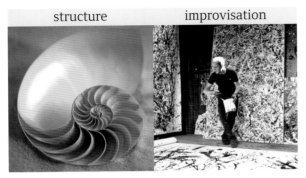

structure | improvisation

art[1] (art) *n.* The conscious production or arrangement of sounds, colors, forms, movements, or other elements in a manner that affects the sense of beauty; specifically, the production of the beautiful in a graphic or plastic medium.
—*The American Heritage Dictionary of the English Language*

In the creative process, you cannot both observe and participate in an event. Your attempt to observe the event while participating will taint your participation; likewise, if you try to participate while being an observer, you lose objectivity. As a result, you have to decide to either watch or play, knowing that you cannot have full knowledge of both.

Another way to look at this phenomenon is that you are either in the bubble or out; prior to the event, you commit to stand outside and observe, comment, critique. You must remain in this realm to really observe what is going on. If you choose to enter the bubble, your conscious critique of the event distorts the groove.

In my world of improvisation, this means that after great preparation ("Chance prefers the prepared mind"—Louis Pasteur), you have to let go of the conscious brain, surrender to the moment, step into the bubble, participate, and be in the *now*.

For me, this duality also occurs in the brain, between the right and left sides. There are two very different thought processes going on, two different ways of perceiving: the cognitive and the intuitive. To shut out one requires a certain amount of self-discipline and practice. If you let the two mix, then you often get "mush," confusion.

If I had learned to draw better, I would never have gotten into sound. —C. Bates

Dissolving the Problem

Perhaps this is my Piscean dilemma—the two fishes forever caught in a quandary of circular confusion. If I do A, I cannot do B, or vice versa.

But I have also found that, in the end, the solution is in neither A nor B, but the invention of C, which, in turn, dissolves the A-B problem. This often requires turning away from the problem as stated and looking elsewhere in logically illogical places: combining physics with economics or biology with structural engineering or, in my case, architecture with jazz.

This may also be the solution to Heisenberg's dilemma. The answer is not in knowing the position and the speed simultaneously, but in approaching the problem from an entirely different perspective. Perhaps it is on one of the seven planes of consciousness discussed in ancient Indian philosophy. Or perhaps it is on one of the ten planes that String Theory currently proposes. (Or the realization that these two conceptual models, one in science and one in philosophy, are, in fact, referring to the same thing.)

Psychologists tell us that our conscious mind makes up less than ten percent of our total brain. Intuition is the connection to the unconscious mind.

In the creative process, you cannot both observe and participate in an event.

To access more of the brain, you can't look it "straight in the eye"; you have to sneak around it, you have to "dance with the unconscious." It's definitely a partnering on all levels—physical, social, and intellectual. The trick is to learn to dance ever closer to the fire without falling headfirst into the flames.

Lastly, I love reading artists' biographies. I love learning about what influenced a certain artwork or idea, because it is often not what popular opinion holds. For example, Marcel Duchamp's interest in the newly developed X-ray photography and in public carnivals influenced the layout of his seminal work, *The Large Glass*. Bob Dylan's "Like a Rolling Stone," considered one of the greatest songs of contemporary music, was first written as a lazy-tempo waltz. It is interesting to me to see how real life intercedes and alters artistic ideas.

All of which brings me to my work: Having been trained as an architect and a jazz musician, I have tried to fuse these two seemingly unrelated disciplines. At times, I find I am attempting to make architecture more spontaneous, more "alive," in the moment. Other projects reverse the paradigm—trying to make music more visual, more physical.

So for all the interested parties, here are some of the influences on my work and philosophy, as told in my language of text and image:

Read the text only and get the straight story;
Read the images only and get a not-so-straight story;
Read the text and the images together, and you may get the real story.

Marcel Duchamp, *The Bride Stripped Bare by Her Bachelors, Even (The Large Glass)*.
Oil, varnish, lead foil, lead wire, and dust on two glass panels, 1915-1923.

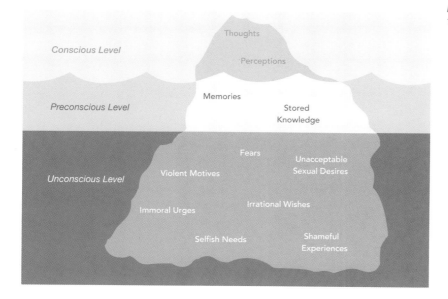

Freud's View of the Human Mind: The Mental Iceberg.

I'm sure Freud helped a great many people, but he also screwed up a lot of people too. It was the fifties and he was the panacea of the decade. Psychoanalysis is powerful stuff; to ask the conscious mind to grasp it all is something my Eastern friends get a good chuckle over. But, nevertheless, this image has always helped me to consider visually what we "know," what we can "control," and what is beyond our conscious mind. It was concepts like this that led me to Transcendental Meditation, Ram Dass, the Eastern perspective, and meditation as a way of "surrendering into the unconscious."
(Illustration © 2005 Pearson Education, Inc.)

When I was eight and my only brother, Peter, was eleven, we were interested in any powered mechanical object—model cars, train sets, gas-powered model airplanes. At a certain moment, we dreamed of actually being *in* the gas-powered object—so was born the idea of owning a go-kart.

Peter and I bothered our parents way too much about it. They finally relented and spent $105.00 on a Royal Norseman from Sears, with a Briggs and Stratton four-cycle engine. We had a long, steep driveway, so we had plenty of room to cruise around. My mom, who was not "gizmo oriented" (as my dad used to say), was unsure of the purchase.

My dad justified it by saying:

1. We were not watching television.
2. We were outside.
3. We were learning to drive.
4. We were learning about engines and mechanics.

We justified it by knowing we were moving faster than we could run, and it was far more dangerous.

I close my eyes in order to see.
—Paul Gaugin

My First Love/Fear Relationship

Needless to say, the "need for speed" was a powerful adolescent force, so Peter and I quickly graduated to a more powerful go-kart, a Simplex Challenger with "racing slicks" (big tires). We also graduated to a more intense sibling rivalry. Soon, we disagreed (and fought) on so many issues that the family worked it out by allowing me to get a second go-kart. When I went to pick it out, it was similar in every way to Peter's, except for the engine. My options were either a wimpy Briggs, a Clinton two-stroke, or the new McCollough MC-7 chain-saw engine with fuel injection. The desire was too much. I had to have this bright yellow, *very loud*, obnoxious-sounding machine. (Think of the sound of chain saws in the quiet, rural wilderness.) This new "wild thing" that I had loved and controlled within limits in its previous incarnation, had now gone "rogue." It was too loud and too fast. It took forever to start and when it did, it drove me. Without intending to, I had created a monster. It was my first love/fear relationship, but not my last.

Soon, the fear overtook the love. I "outgrew" the go-kart and moved on to a louder and more obnoxious machine that didn't move as fast, the drums.

...the "need for speed" was a powerful adolescent force.

Dad justified it by saying:
we were not watching television
we were outside
we were learning to drive
we were learning about engines and mechanics

Drum

The Permanent Sound of Excavation

In 1963, I was thirteen, and rock and roll was in full swing. I had been singing to all of Elvis's, Ricky Nelson's, and Ray Charles's records. I had started and stopped piano lessons too many times. I knew I loved music, but the *Hanon Piano Exercises* and memorizing written notes on a page, as taught by some elderly woman with thick glasses, was not what I considered "music." I bombed big time every week at the lesson.

So, when a few classmates who played guitar and piano wanted to start a band and they said they needed a drummer, I thought this was more my kind of music. I innocently asked my dad at dinner one night if I could get a set of drums. He replied, "You mean like Gene Krupa?" ("Who the hell is Gene Krupa?" I wondered.)

"Right," I replied.

What I didn't know was that all that swinging, syncopated music by Benny Goodman and Ella Fitzgerald that I had been hearing at home was Gene Krupa or Lou Bellson on the drums. (I soon found out that my dad had a standing order with the local music store—"Any Goodman or Ella record comes in, please send over a copy.") So, unbeknownst to me, I was quite knowledgeable on swing-era music and could easily scat from memory Gene Krupa's "Sing, Sing, Sing."

Christopher Janney, *Burning Drum*.
Wood, velvet, aluminum, 1982.
Reading Joseph Campbell's book, *The Power of Myth*, I discovered the Shiva image, which took on a special meaning for me. In one hand, Shiva holds a drum, the "drum of time." I understood this to mean that all forms have rhythm—they are vibrating at the molecular level. In the other hand, Shiva holds "the flame." Fire signifies a means of transformation, the ability to burn away the old, allowing the new to arise.

I took one of my old snare drums and burned it. Cross-breeding between music and visual art, I added a paint brush and a drum brush in a painter's can. Then I created a "coffin" for the piece in dark blue velvet. I took the piece with me when I lectured. It was not my new musical instrument, but my new "instrument about music."

The next night my dad and I went to a musical instrument store and purchased a set of gold metal-flake drums (no cymbals). As we loaded the drums into the house, I remember him saying with resignation, "I bet we will be donating these to your school in three months."

How was it that I was sick at 7:30 the very next morning? Everyone went off to work or school and by 8:30, I was pounding away in the basement, playing along to my Elvis, Ricky Nelson, and Ray Charles records.

Over the next two years, every spare moment—after school until 7 p.m. dinner, after homework, Saturday morning, Sunday—I was on the drums. My mom referred to it as "the permanent sound of excavation."

The band practiced in my basement on weekends. We covered everything from a simplified version of Ray's "What'd I Say" to Elvis's version of "Hound Dog" to the Kingsmen's version of "Louie, Louie" and not much else. But, more importantly, we had a name—a band is not a band without a name. The guitar player said he had heard of this "cool" place down at Rehoboth Beach called the the Zen Den. Mmm, the Zens, we thought, that's a cool sound. So, with absolutely no "conscious" awareness of the derivation, the Zens were born.

Christopher Janney, *Percussion-Discussion*.
Drums, electronics, interactive, 1981.
All spoken words in any language have pitch and rhythm. So, I set about creating a piece that would explore this "hidden music"in language— I built a set of "talking drums," playing with the idea between cognition and sound.

Throughout high school and college, I played in a lot of bands, all based in rock and soul. But the music became less about "covering" the tunes and more about improvisation, especially on the instrumental breaks. Living in Washington, DC, had also exposed me to more rhythm and blues and soul music than jazz or hard rock. I went to the Howard Theater many times to see "The Tall, Talented, Temptin' Temptations," Otis Redding, Sam and Dave, Marvin Gaye, and the "Godfather of Soul," James Brown. DC was a great scene for R&B. I watched the drummers like a hawk and then went home, put on the tunes, and tried to find that elusive groove.

Some of my best musical experiences occurred when my band would play a dance party. I could feel the interaction between us and the people dancing. We would feed off their movement energy, which would push us to wilder improvisations (or quieter, softer, raunchier). Our change of tempo or energy, in turn, would push them to dance wildly and more creatively. At fourteen years of age, this was a great experience of music, movement, group energy, communal interaction.

I think most kids are [ritualistic]. Eager to gain some control over their lives, they concoct games and rites to add sense and form to their world.
—Twyla Tharp

Early Dance/Music Improvisations

I continued to play in bands through high school, with ever-looser musical structures. As the popular Zeitgeist evolved, so did the rest of us. The Beatles went from the tight AABA form of "She Loves You," to a more open structure, to the whole concept album of *Sargent Pepper's Lonely Hearts Club Band*. Dylan created such intertwined lyrics as in "Like A Rolling Stone." Miles Davis's *Bitches Brew* and John Coltrane's *A Love Supreme* gave the rest of us the freedom to let go, loosen up, and get in the moment, dance party or no dance party.

But playing at the parties, playing for people, was still the "hit" for me. Later on, in my twenties, I played more and more concerts, eventually playing a 1974 date at Lincoln Center in New York when my current band, Orion, won a jazz competition. It was a nice honor, but it wasn't as good as playing the dance party in a Soho loft afterwards.

Christopher Janney, *Sonic Forest: Bonnaroo*. Light, sound, aluminum, interactive, 2005. "I loved the *Sonic Forest*. In the morning it was the place to hang and have a coffee while listening to exotic birds. In the afternoon it was a great place to meet up with friends or take a nap (when you shut your eyes you were in an enchanted forest). At night, after the last band, we would meet there and dance for hours to the continuous drum jams on into the early morning." —Ashley Capps, Bonnaroo Co-producer

I grew up in Washington, DC, until the age of fifteen. My dad worked for the Central Intelligence Agency and my mom was a school teacher at the Potomac School, an elementary school for grades four through nine. Since she was a teacher there, it was decided that that's where I would go to school after third grade. Most of my friends went to the other all-boys schools around DC—St. Albans, Landon, St. Stephen's. When I first entered Potomac, it felt like a raw deal. I was pissed. I was not in the testosterone-charged environment of an all-boys school with my other friends. However, within a year, I knew this was the school for me. I was in an environment with girls, which I later realized was a far more normal and healthy circumstance for me than a single-sex school. We had art and music every day—at least that's how I remember it. And we had one of the best music educators in the country teaching us, a man named Jack Langstaff. We sang in school productions, and when the Washington Opera Company needed child singers, they called Jack.

In the early fall of 1963, Jack missed several weeks of school. We asked our other teachers where he was, and were told he had gone to England to work on an album of folk songs. Upon his return, I remember asking him what he had done in England, and he told me he had been making a record. He went on to remark that when he was rehearsing in the studio, the producer kept having these four other musicians come in to listen to his American accent and his enunciation. A few months later, the Beatles stormed America, and Jack said one day, so nonchalantly, "Those are the four guys who were in my studio."

Due to Jack's influence, I have always sung. Perhaps it is not music that everyone would agree is interesting, but I find there is no substitute for this "original instrument" when it comes to creating spontaneity, releasing energy, and expressing oneself. I realize now how much of my approach to music and creativity was shaped by being around Jack with his joie de vivre.

Christopher Janney/Susan Cooper,
The Dark and the Light.
Light, sound, performance, 1989.

> For the 1989 Christmas Revels concert, Jack asked Susan and me to create a grand finale. We started with the archetypal idea of a doomsday that leads into darkness. I scored a six-channel surround-sound piece for the Sanders Theater and designed a giant sun that went into an eclipse. It only passed when the audience sang "Dona Nobis Pacem" as a three-part canon. In this final movement. I had the crew in the rafters sprinkling down slivers of gold mylar, "pieces of new light," onto the audience.

The creator of the new composition in the arts is an outlaw until he is a classic. —Gertrude Stein

Jack Langstaff / Sir George Martin

After the Potomac School, I lost touch with Jack for many years. It wasn't until 1976, when I was in Boston at MIT, that I ran into him on the street. He was living there, teaching, and had started The Revels, an extraordinary annual songfest and performance celebrating the winter solstice. We stayed in touch and occassionally worked together.

One afternoon in 1998, Jack called me up in my studio in Lexington and asked if I was "terribly busy." He added, "I have some friends here I would like to bring out to your studio for a visit." An hour or so later, Jack arrived by car and out stepped Sir George Martin, producer of the Beatles, and his wife, Lady Judy. *That is so Jack!* We spent the whole afternoon together, walking around my studio, talking about ideas of music, architecture, recording, the rhythm of life.

George's pioneering work has been an inspiration to my generation, and it is a great gift to have him as a friend. On the one hand, he is the producer who has been responsible for some of the most creative music of my generation, but he is also a person always interested and willing to listen to what new possibilities might arise. We've had some long lunches exchanging ideas on music and architecture,

For the hell of it, I asked Giles if I could hear just the harmony track of Paul singing on "I Want to Hold Your Hand," circa 1964. Giles punched it up and a rush of memories as a fourteen-year-old flooded my imagination.

Christopher Janney and Sir George Martin at Abbey Road Studios.

always coming back to Beethovan, Bach, and their "cathedrals of sound." We talked often of the reality of the music business driving the creativity now, hopeful that the pendulum will swing back.

In 2006, I had a treat one day when George and I were together in London. He mentioned that he and his son, producer Giles Martin, were working on a Beatles score for a Cirque du Soleil production. Their task was to create a running collage of Beatles songs and transitions. I ended up back at Abbey Road Studios with them, listening to the work in progress. We were in a small post-production studio with all the original Beatles tracks unmixed. I asked Giles if I could hear just the harmony track of Paul singing on "I Want to Hold Your Hand," circa 1964. Giles punched it up and a rush of memories as a fourteen-year-old flooded my imagination.

But what was even more interesting was what they were doing with the music. Rather than taking entire songs, George and Giles were constructing parts: crossfading, reversing, overlapping. It was a rich palette of music history, and they were creating this incredible pastiche: an "impressionist canvas" of emotions and memorable "audicons" (audio icons), interwoven into a huge collage of sonic portraits.

The first two years of college were a time to experiment and see what truly interested me. I had drawn industrial objects, made models, and was interested in architecture for as long as I could remember. Architecture seemed to represent a nice "middle of the road" creative endeavor—not too way-out, but with room for creativity. I also thought I could possibly get a job when I got out of college. *Wrong.* In the late seventies, "urban sociology" was all the rage in architecture, and Princeton led the pack.

To add to my educational confusion, the spring of 1970 was a tumultuous time for me—there were the nationwide school strikes against the war in Vietnam, the abolishment of the draft, and the institution of the lottery; there were certain experiments with psychedelic drugs; there was my improvisational music. It was all moving too fast, with many more questions than answers. I went to my parents and asked if I could drop out of college for a year. (My lottery number was 354, so there was no chance of being drafted into the military.) They replied, "As long as you get a job and support yourself, it's your call."

I ended up in Boston, doing a number of activities throughout the year—playing in a few different bands, and working odd jobs—as a dishwasher and busboy in a French restaurant, painting houses, and working construction. In my spare time, I started making visual art. At one point, I was so into painting, I decided to put my white bed sheets up on the wall and paint big abstract colored forms on them with acrylics and magic markers. Lots of primary colors. I then had the bright idea to put the sheets back on the bed and sleep in them. All this seemed like an "immersively" good idea, until I woke up the next morning with paint and permanent magic marker all over my body. I had sweated in the night, which had caused the colors to transfer to my skin. I was "tattooed" for a few days.

Pruitt-Igoe, built 1956, destroyed 1972.

Le Corbusier, *Notre Dame du Haut.*
Reinforced concrete, 1956.

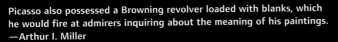

Picasso also possessed a Browning revolver loaded with blanks, which he would fire at admirers inquiring about the meaning of his paintings.
—Arthur I. Miller

Painting my Bed Sheets

"I must study politics and war that my sons may have liberty to study mathematics and philosophy. My sons ought to study mathematics and philosophy, geography, natural history, naval architecture, navigation, commerce, and agriculture... in order to give their children a right to study painting, poetry, music, architecture, statuary, tapestry, and porcelain."

John Adams, 1781

Wassily Kandinsky, *Improvisation 31*.
Oil on canvas, 1913.

Kandinsky was considered by many to be the father of abstract art; he was also a musician. It is known that he drew quite intensively on his musical ideas, trying to tap directly into his unconscious and intuition, when generating his early abstract compositions.

Christopher Janney, *Environment Study*, 1974.

Casting about for ways to manifest my thoughts on creating artwork "with nature," I designed this painting to float on the surface of a swimming pool in the month of October. Hoping fall winds would transform this rectilinear piece into a more chaotic composition, my idea was to photograph the work for three days and document the transformation. As it turned out, there was very little wind, and at first, I was disappointed. But slowly, as leaves fell into the piece, it was altered in a way I hadn't imagined.

Christopher Janney, *Resonating Frequencies: 3D Study.*
Powdered resin, 2003.

Thought-forms about merging two into one; playing visually with the Piscean problem. Sometimes,
it becomes a solution looking for a problem.
Here, I was asked to create a logo for my
"Resonating Frequencies." I began thinking about
the disciplines of architecture and music rubbing
against one another. Trying to push the two
together—consider the heat, the friction, the
sweat, the vibrations. I looked up on my wall and
there was this study I had made a year earlier.

[Einstein] thought of both musical and physical truths as Platonic forms that the mind must intuit.
Great music cannot be "created" any more than great physics can be deduced strictly from experimental
data. Some aestheic sense of the universe is necessary for both. —Arthur I. Miller

Peripheral Vision

I was very fortunate to have many great professors in college, including graphic
artist Carol Bankerd, architect Lance Brown, architect Harrison Fraker, architect
Michael Graves, art critic Rosalind Krauss, and electronic sculptor James Seawright.

While at Princeton, I worked on and off in Graves's office because I wanted to
see how an architect's office functioned. Graves also knew of my love of music and
sometimes came to hear my bands play. I recall a conversation with him about my
interest in both music and architecture. He replied, "You will have to choose
between the two. You can't do both."

At various times in my life, I thought about making the choice. But the conscious "choosing" seemed so inconsequential. To "choose" one or the other seemed
somehow to let the small conscious mind overpower the vast subconscious. It felt
more natural to continue to work on what sincerely interested me and to trust my
intuition. I wanted to let the choosing happen in an unconscious moment, and do
whatever I had to do to make a living and allow this path to unfold over time.

Christopher Janney, *A House Is a Musical Instrument: Lexington,* Living Room studies, 2003.

Computer modeling has transformed the design process. However, it does not take the place of freehand drawing—the immediate flow of ideas from eye to hand. I often begin with drawing or making some sort of 3-D, physical paper model. From there, ideas go into the computer to be clarified, refined. Sometimes, I take the computer drawings and draw on top of them, then put it all back in the computer. It is important not to let this sexy electronic medium beckon me into something *it* wants to draw as opposed to what my clunky, but free, intuition is trying to manifest.

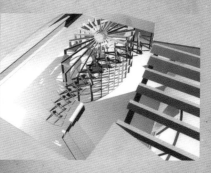

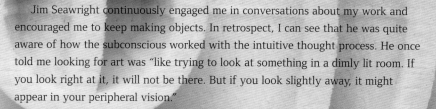

Jim Seawright continuously engaged me in conversations about my work and encouraged me to keep making objects. In retrospect, I can see that he was quite aware of how the subconscious worked with the intuitive thought process. He once told me looking for art was "like trying to look at something in a dimly lit room. If you look right at it, it will not be there. But if you look slightly away, it might appear in your peripheral vision."

Creating physical objects seemed as natural to me as drawing. I discovered there was something to learn through the actual building of a model or mock-up of a design that could not be learned through drawing. Going back and forth between the two was even better; the sketch model could further develop the drawing, and then redrawing the design based on this information often generated stimulating dialogue.

I recall a conversation with Carol Bankerd around this time. In an effort to get me to focus on just one medium, one material, she asked why I had to try so many different things at once. I replied, "These are the first things I think about when I wake up in the morning—that moment when you are not fully awake, but you are rested. You know you won't go back to sleep, so you lie there and think whatever you want with a lucid mind. And that's what I imagine: some synthesis of these ideas and materials, somewhere in real space, real time."

In 1973, living in New York, I continued to pursue my interests in architecture, art, and music. I had met Gary Zeller, the president of The Plastics Factory, at Pratt Institute, where I took some courses. I then landed a job working for his company, building sets for theater, television, and trade shows. During the days, I learned the trade, building sets with professional carpenters and fabricators, while at night I rehearsed with different bands and occasionally performed in clubs. On off-nights, I stayed in and read books on art, performance, and architecture.

I recall reading a book on avant-garde artists that included John Cage, Merce Cunningham, and Marcel Duchamp. In the section on Merce, it described him creating a performance with Frank Stella as the set designer. In the book it stated, "Then Merce turned to his technical director Gary Zeller and discussed the fabrication issues." I was momentarily shocked. Could this be the same Gary Zeller for whom I had been working for over two months? I went into work the next day with the book. Smiling, Gary replied, "Don't start with me about Merce." Over lunch breaks and after work, I continually bothered Gary about Cunningham, and consequently learned a great deal about how certain of Merce's greatest works, like *Walkaround Time*, his homage to Duchamp, were actually conceived, developed, and executed.

From then on, Gary assigned me to any artist-related projects the company worked on. One day he came back to me in the shop and said the artist Jack Youngerman was up front, and did I want to help him load some materials into his car. I knew of Jack's paintings but was not aware of his sculpture. I introduced myself to him and asked what he was making. We talked a bit about his new direction in making fiberglass sculptures and the process. I asked if I could come out to his studio in Bridgehampton some weekend and see the work. Two weeks later, I went out to visit and ended up working with Jack for the next five years.

Merce Cunningham, *Antic Meet*, John Cage, composer, 1958.

I remember seeing Merce and his company for the first time in 1972. With much of the dance in silence, I could "see" the music. Similarly, John Cage's music made its own visual images. I called what they were doing "separate integrities."
I read that Merce and John would agree on a subject, and then each would go away and create a work: Merce, a dance; John, the music. They would not rehearse the two together, but would allow the two performances to coincide for the first time on opening night. The audience would see a dance and hear music composed about the same idea—a strange brand of synaesthesia, but one which kept the informed viewer on the edge of his thought-provoking seat.

I like to surprise myself; that is my guarantee to surprise others. —Joe Zawinul

Constructive Knowledge

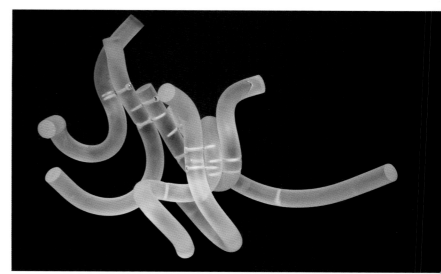

Christopher Janney, *Form Studies*. Acrylic, 2001.
Working between musical improvisation and physical colored form, I have utilized different materials at different times. Here I was working with the one-inch diameter clear cast acrylic rod, which I cut up in sections and heated in an oven. I then had about twenty minutes to "jam," to shape them into various configurations and play with the visual rhythms. They were studies both for larger physical works and for musical compositions.

Jack Youngerman, *Black Juba*.
Fiberglass, 1980.

Working for Jack on and off for five years, I was allowed to see into the world of a professional artist. I remember once repairing one of his sculptures in the studio next to where he was working. He had been talking on the phone and shuffling some tables around. At a certain moment, I realized I had not heard a sound for a good fifteen minutes. I quietly walked around the corner and saw him focused on a new painting—experimenting with different colors within the forms. The phone was off the hook and all the doors to the outside were closed. It was as if he needed the absolute least amount of distraction to coax his muse out, to move very slowly and just observe what might appear. I sat there quietly for more than half an hour, observing his process and intense concentration.

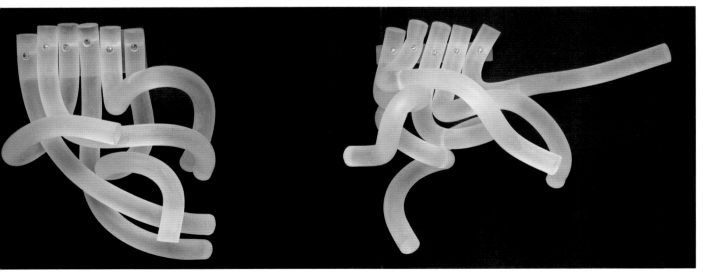

153

While living in New York, I continued to read more books on art, go to galleries, museums, and performances, and soak up the art and architecture scene. This caused me to think more about the stability of the "architecture profession" versus the "what life?" of an artist. For artists, I thought there just wasn't any "there" there. However, slowly, art became a physical entity to me, particularly as I read more about Marcel Duchamp. One night, it struck me that art can be as present as a building; it just has an ever-changing, ever-transforming physical form. Sometimes it could be manifested in paint, sometimes in concrete, but, when it is good, when you are looking at/listening to/touching/smelling/tasting it, it is a very tangible thing.

For me, it was Duchamp who continuously stripped away the utility and laid bare the essence. I read that Duchamp once said, "A title is like an invisible color." With his works *L.H.O.O.Q.* and *Fresh Widow* especially, I could see how the title framed or extended the idea, and how Duchamp was always pushing for synaesthetic events—events where more than one sense was at work, be it the eyes and the intellect or, as in *With Hidden Noise*, eyes, sound, concept. So, it wasn't too much of a leap when I realized how sound within a visual environment could also be this "invisible color" that could add another new layer to the visual or architectural information. From there, it becomes an interplay of media, pushing the viewer/participant to the level of their choice.

Marcel Duchamp, *L.H.O.O.Q.*
Drawing on photographic reproduction, 1919.

Marcel Duchamp, *With Hidden Noise.*
Metal, string, sound, 1916.

By 1916 Duchamp had stopped "painting." He was casting about for other ways to express art than through retinal means. From the Ready-Mades to the *Roto-reliefs* to *The Large Glass*, all were in play. *With Hidden Noise* opened the idea to me that "sound is a visual medium." An object does not have to have physical form to be physically visible. The physical form is in the mind of the viewer.

Designers solve problems. Artists ask questions.
—S.A. Moi

Sound is an Invisible Color

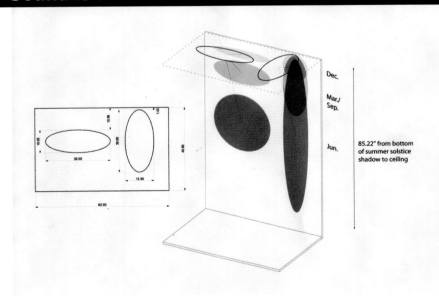

Dec.

Mar./
Sep.

Jun.

85.22" from bottom
of summer solstice
shadow to ceiling

Christopher Janney, *Sidereal Time.*
Aluminum, electronics, light, 1998.

Always interested in "big rhythms," I designed both this double-ellipse skylight and the Sun/Moon clock to manifest these rhythms. This clock and skylight are together in the foyer of my Lexington, Massachusetts, house.

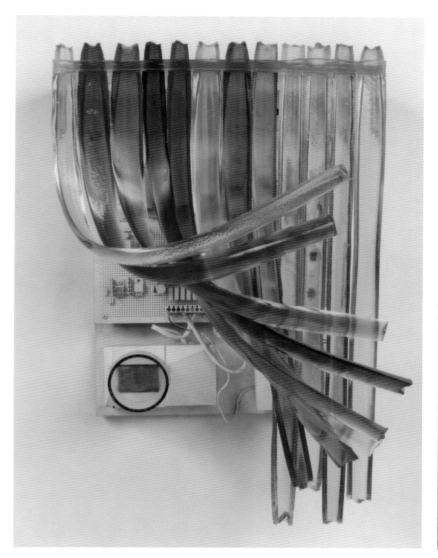

Christopher Janney, *Sound Is an Invisible Color.*
Colored resin, electronics, sound, 1989.

> For many years in the eighties, I continued to
> create a series of colored sculptures, exploring my
> interest in color and transparency. Concurrently,
> I had been building interactive sound environ-
> ments. In an effort to fuse these two interests in
> form and sound, I started creating a series of
> "combo studies." I titled the whole series
> *Sound Is an Invisible Color* after Duchamp's
> statement, "A title is an invisible color."

Christopher Janney, *Turn Up the Heat,*
American Airlines Arena Scoreboard, Miami.
Aluminum, electronics, light, sound, interactive, 2000.

Le Corbusier/Varèse/Xénakis, *Poeme Electronique.*
Brussels World's Fair, 1958.

> This structure has stood as one of the great
> experimentations in architecture and sound.
> Phillips Corporation commissioned architect
> Le Corbusier to design the building. Le Corbusier,
> in turn, asked Edgard Varèse to be the composer.
> Architect/composer Xénakis was working in
> Le Corbusier's office at the time and was the
> project manager. In hindsight, it is clearly
> Xénakis's design and Varèse's music with a
> 456-speaker sound environment. Le Corbusier
> was actually more concerned with the
> "processional event," having composed the
> visual imagery and experience for the public
> as they moved through the space.

During the seventies, when I lived in New York, I had often admired the work of Isamu Noguchi, who lived in New York as well. I wanted to meet him and talk to him about my work. One Thursday morning, I opened up the phone book and looked up his name, "Noguchi I." There it was. What's the worst he could say, "No?" So I dialed the number. (Now I remember what those early teenage dating years were like: stomach in knots, stuttering, sweaty palms, confused intentions.)

He answered the phone. I introduced myself, stated that I had recently graduated from Princeton in architecture and visual arts, I greatly admired his work, and I wondered if I could come by and talk with him about my work (yes, all in one breath). A pause. "How about 10 a.m. Saturday?" My reply, "No problem."

I went to his Upper East Side apartment that following Saturday with my tray of slides. The door opened and there Noguchi stood in his bathrobe. "Hello, come in." No smile. He was finishing a bowl of cereal in the kitchen and asked me to wait in the living room. The phone rang. From the conversation, I could tell it was the mother of Gordon Matta-Clark. Gordon was an artist in the early seventies who had gone to Cornell architecture school. Upon graduation, he started cutting out sections of old condemned houses—say a four-by-four-foot section of a window and wall, or a three-by-three-foot section of a floor threshold. He would then mount them on pedestals. At that time, he was exhibiting his work at the Holly Solomon Gallery.

Judging from Noguchi's end of the conversation, Gordon's mother was upset with what her son was doing. Noguchi said he would go take a look at the work and then talk to Gordon about his destructive ways.

Noguchi reappeared and asked if I minded if we took a drive. He had to look at a rug at Modern Tapestries that had been created from his drawing. My answer, "No problem." He had a little VW and we drove down to 57th Street. We walked

Christopher Janney, *Light Waves*.
Glass, aluminium, and sound, 2001.

Using the sunlight to "paint the building." Since there is no more powerful light source than the sun, don't fight it, use it as a light source—better yet, as a kinetic (ever-moving) light source. This was an idea I began to consider in college, making colored plexiglas paintings and hanging them out my window. With the "mask of the night, " using artificial light, I can then create an entirely different kind of work. After all, people tend to be different in the light than they are in the dark—why not art?

Art History is to artists as Ornithology is to the birds.
—Barnett Newman

A Day With Noguchi

into the gallery and there was a polite hush. I shadowed him. We were escorted to the back storage racks. They pulled out this twelve-by-fifteen-foot rug, white with a black line drawing on it; it looked like a giant sketch. They asked Noguchi what he thought. He looked quietly for a moment and then turned to me and asked, "What do you think?" This was about the fifteenth word he had spoken to me since we had met. Thinking fast, I replied, "Yes, it's interesting. Does it have a title?"

Noguchi replied, "Let's call it *Drawing for an Absent Sculpture*." So that's how the big dogs title their work.

We then got back in the car and drove downtown to the Holly Solomon Gallery, off to fulfill mother Matta-Clark's wishes. We walked into the gallery, and there were about six or eight sections of buildings on pedestals—worn floorboards, cheap wallpaper next to peeling paint on an old window. Noguchi walked around slowly, then said, "He's got something here." I wondered how was he going to appease both Gordon's mother and support Gordon's cutting up buildings.

We hopped back in the car and drove to Long Island City to a big warehouse.

Isamu Noguchi, *Worksheet for Sculpture.*
Black craft paper and graphite on graph paper, 1945-46.
Noguchi was a great inspiration for me. He worked as a sculptor, a set designer, and a landscape designer. Consider the different scales involved. Of all his work, his stage sets for Martha Graham are what I love most: "... to wed the total void of theater space to form and action... space became a volume to be dealt with sculpturally."

(In the early seventies, Long Island City was a major industrial ghetto.) We parked, walked to a large concrete building, went up some stairs and through a huge industrial door. There in front of me were about fifty Noguchi sculptures laid out in a 10,000 square-foot loft space. I had died and gone to heaven.

As we walked down through the space, each one was different. There was no "style," no particularly continuous idea that I could see in the work. I remarked how there was so much variety. He replied, "They're all just experiments, really. Trying new things each time." We then came to a second door. He opened it and looked out on a garden, an outdoor space with another ten or fifteen pieces. I was

overwhelmed and muttered something about his use of outdoor space. No reply.

We then went downstairs to a series of drawing studios. I noticed a door in the hallway next to his door. It read "Buckminster Fuller Designs." *Hello.*

I asked, "Does Buckminster Fuller also work here?"

"Yes, when he is in New York. We are old friends."

Imagine Mr. Dymaxion Geodesic Dome and Mr. Natural hanging out together.

We went into one of Noguchi's drawing studios, where he had a slide projector. Time to show my work. I loaded up the slides and took him through my embryonic work, struggling to sound intelligent. We spent most of the time on one maquette of a piece I had designed for the side of a twenty-story building on 23rd Street. It had large rings of transparent colored acrylic attached to the south-facing side of the building, creating a giant "colored shadow painting".

I remarked how I didn't have all the structural issues resolved and might have to add cables for stability.

He replied, "That might make it more interesting." We talked a bit more, then drove back to the city and parted ways.

Christopher Janney, *Light/Shadow*, study.
Photo montage, 1973.

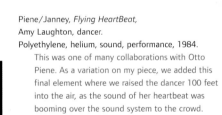

After three years in New York, I was pretty broke and burnt out. I knew the normal architecture graduate school track was not going to be satisfying. I had seen the possibilities of artists who built architectural projects—Isamu Noguchi, Claes Oldenburg, Otto Piene—and saw this as a more desirable path. At this point, I also had played enough music in clubs, studios, and on tours to realize that performing music exclusively as a drummer was not going to be my life. But I knew music was never going to leave me alone.

Coincidentally, the German environmental artist Otto Piene had recently become Director of the Center for Advanced Visual Studies, a research center that was part of MIT's School of Architecture. I took a trip to Cambridge to visit with him and discuss the idea of studying there. He told me that the center was starting a small graduate program and I should apply. I was accepted and, the next fall, moved to Boston.

I studied and worked at MIT for the next ten years as a research fellow (there are no "artists" at MIT). Within my first semester there, I realized that there were engineers, scientists, and students who could build anything I could imagine. So, I pursued my role as an artist in this community, dreaming up the most creative ideas I could without paying too much attention as to how they might be built. I would then seek out the talent in this community to help me realize them. From my early projects of *Soundstair*, to *Percussion-Discussion* (actual English-speaking drums), to *HeartBeat*, they all were conceived and produced by me, but built by others in collaboration with me who were better equipped at whatever physical discipline was necessary—electrical, mechanical, chemical, astrophysical, etc.

All these people who helped me build my projects—engineers, scientists, machinists, musicians—have imaginations too. I found out the hard way that the less clear the initial idea, the more other people influence and often dilute the

Piene/Janney, *Flying HeartBeat*,
Amy Laughton, dancer.
Polyethylene, helium, sound, performance, 1984.
This was one of many collaborations with Otto Piene. As a variation on my piece, we added this final element where we raised the dancer 100 feet into the air, as the sound of her heartbeat was booming over the sound system to the crowd.

The professional keeps his eye on the doughnut and not on the hole. He reminds himself it's better to be in the arena, getting stomped by the bull, than to be in the stands or out in the parking lot. —Steven Pressfield

Artist/Engineer/Consultant

concept. So, as the artist, my role is not only to conceive of the idea, but to keep the idea on track.

During the 1980s, I worked for many artists, including Claes Oldenberg, Jack Youngerman and Robert Morris. It seemed like I did most of the work, actually building their sculptures. But here it would be important to quote Thomas Edison: "Genius is one percent inspiration and ninety-nine percent perspiration." Having worked on both sides of this equation, it is true that ninety-nine percent is almost all of the work, but if there isn't that spark, that single thought, that one percent, there is no fire, no art.

Jack Youngerman, *Dryad*.
Laminated wood, steel, 1983.

Jack Youngerman was the artist with whom I worked the longest. From building his thirty-foot fiberglass sculpture for Pittsburgh in 1977 to the creation of numerous fiberglass pieces, to the creation of the seventy-five-foot Dryad in 1983 for Neiman-Marcus, the construction problems were some of the most challenging and most interesting I faced. Ultimately, I knew I had to step away from this world of form and find a way to reinterpret this energy through my use of the medium of sound.

Jack Youngerman
working on sculptural form, 1978.

Christopher Janney in the
Youngerman studio, 1978.

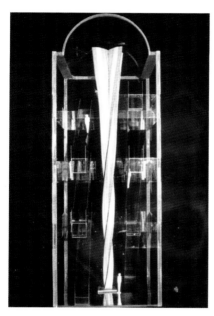

Claes Oldenburg, *Popcorn*, study.
Foam, wire, 1985.

Having access to the resources of MIT, Claes asked me how I might be able to scale up a piece of popcorn so that he might study it more closely. Fellow artist Geoff Pingree and I devised a method of slicing the original popcorn into .005-inch cross-sections using a biology lab "microtome." We photographed each section, then enlarged the images on twenty-four-by-twenty-four-inch photo-paper, cut them out, and glued them together, creating a 3-D landscape of popcorn. When we showed it to Claes, he replied, "Oh, I didn't think you could make it that real."

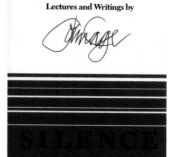

John Cage, *Silence*, 1961.

Susan Schwartzenberg, The Exploratorium, John Cage portrait, 1987.

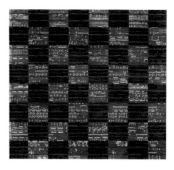

John Cage, *Chess*, 1944.

Both Cage and Duchamp were great lovers of chess. When I played chess with John, it was interesting because it was not a social game to him; I couldn't really engage him in conversation much during the game. I remember playing fairly defensively, reacting to his moves. I knew I wasn't playing that well and felt as if he was looking into my mind as we played. I tried to watch his mind, his patterns, and his focus on the different areas of the board, but, in the end, it was checkmate.

And what is the purpose of writing music?

One is, of course, not dealing with purposes but with sounds. Or the answer must take the form of a paradox: a purposeful purposelessness or a purposeless play. This play, however, is an affirmation of life—not an attempt to bring order out of chaos nor to suggest improvements in creation, but simply a way of waking up to the very life we are living, which is so excellent once one gets one's mind and one's desires out of its way and lets it act of its own accord.

—John Cage

My intention was always to get away from myself, though I knew perfectly well that I was using myself. Call it a little game between "I" and "me." —Marcel Duchamp

John Cage

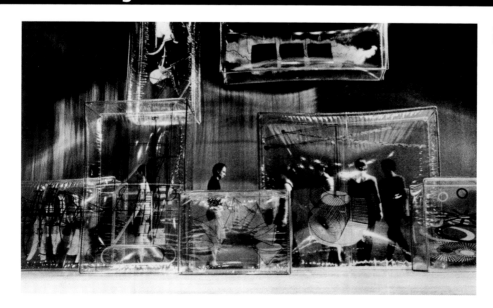

Jasper Johns, set designer, *Walkaround Time*, Merce Cunningham Dance Company, 1968.

Sometime in 1981, I read that there was going to be a performance of Vsevolod Meyerhold's *Magnanimous Cuckold* staged at the Solomon R. Guggenheim Museum, New York, in conjunction with an exhibit on Russian Constructivism. I had always been a huge fan of these artists of the early twentieth century —their mix of machine aesthetics, politics, and "agit-prop" theater, as well as their efforts to bring art into the street and make it relevant to their daily lives.

Just before the performance began, there were two empty seats next to me, and down sat Merce Cunningham and John Cage. So there I sat for a good ninety minutes—watching a reenactment of one of the great early twentieth century performances, with "art royalty" on my right.

At the end of the show, John turned to me and asked me why I came to the show. I explained briefly about my work at MIT. They both seemed interested. John asked if I would come visit with him sometime, talk to him more about my work, and, lastly, he inquired, "Do you play chess?" (I played a great deal with my dad when I was twelve, wondering whatever could I learn from this game.)

I went to visit John a few weeks later in New York, and we talked for a few hours—me mostly asking him questions about performance, music, and sound. We played a game of chess. He won.

At the end of our visit, he announced that Symphony Space was planning a concert for his seventieth birthday and wondered if I would create some sort of piece for the concert. This began a long and interesting friendship with John until his death in 1992.

Christopher Janney, *Sonic Pass Blue*, Lehman College, Bronx, NY. Colored glass, sound, interactive, 1999.

For John's seventieth birthday celebration at Symphony Space in 1983, I created a temporary installation of *Sonic Pass*. I set photosensors along the two main aisles, allowing people's movement patterns to generate the rhythmic content of a score. I then composed a series of flutelike timbres using my Oberheim four-voice synthesizer. The resulting composition was amplified over the house sound system during intermissions. *The New York Times* referred to the sounds as "peaceful polyps" punctuating the din of the crowd.

Ryoanji Garden, Japan, 1488.

Cage created both drawings and music about this Japanese garden starting in 1983. He worked on them until he died in 1992. He had a collection of fifteen rocks that he would use in developing compositions. He said, "I've been using those particular fifteen rocks for many years... There's nothing special about them, other than they are the same fifteen rocks and that's related to the number of stones in the Ryoanji Garden in Tokyo."

"The Architect is responsible to create the spirit of a thought. And to translate it through whatever medium is available, whether it be in a text, in a drawing, in a model, in a building, in a photograph, or in a film. The Architect concerns himself/herself with the mysteries of space and form, and is also obligated to invent new programs. It is essential that the Architect creates works that are thought-provoking and ultimately life-provoking. Or more precisely, life-giving to what appears to be at first inanimate materials. The Architect enters into a social contract in the deepest sense. To search for qualities and human values which give spirit."

John Hejduk, *Wall House 2*, Groningen, the Netherlands. Designed 1973, built 2001.

"The sound of dreams, like the dreams themselves, can be strange. When we awake we are able to capture fragments of the images in our dreams, but we almost never can capture the sound of our dreams. In our journey from painting through literature and then within the body we have crossed over from an open external to a closed internal…"
—J. Hejduk, *Evening in Llano*

As Dean of the Irwin S. Chanin School of Architecture of The Cooper Union, John Hejduk was a revered architect, poet, and educator whom I knew only by reputation when I was in college. In the early seventies, he was part of a group that published a book titled *Five Architects*—Charles Gwathmey, Michael Graves, Peter Eisenman, Richard Meier, and Hejduk. I referred to them as the "Jive Five," partly because I thought the architecture was extremely over-intellectualized.

So, it was with some trepidation in 1983 that I found myself standing in an elevator with John and curator David Ross at the Institute of Contemporary Art

S O U N D I N G S

A WORK BY JOHN HEJDUK

In speaking of Order, [Louis] Kahn called that which does not yet exist, Silence. That which exists, he called Light. Silence is the unmeasurable, the desire to be.
—John Lobell

John Hejduk

in Boston. I was rehearsing for the first performance of *HeartBeat* to be performed there. David introduced us and I stepped out at my floor.

As it turns out, John came to the performance the next day. Afterward, he walked up to me, shook my hand, and said, "If you ever want to teach, call me," and then walked away. It was not until seven years later that I called him to discuss the concept of the teaching profession in general. When his secretary put me through to him, he said, "I remember that performance like it was yesterday." Surely, he had me confused with someone else, but I thanked him and asked if I could come talk with him about teaching at the college level; how my concepts of sound might work in any pedagogical environment, or if they would fit at all.

We met the next week in his office at Cooper Union in New York. He greeted me warmly and reiterated how that performance of *HeartBeat* with Sara Rudner was one of the most beautiful performances he had ever seen. Now I was certain that he had the right guy, but not sure what he saw. So I talked about the genesis of the idea a bit, wondering how to get this discussion around to my questions about teaching in

Problem #2: Create a musical instrument that is part
of an existing or invented ritual.
Ritchie Israel, *The Breath.*
Yevgeniy Verbitskiy, *Indirect Communication.*

any art or architecture school. Soon after, in walked Jay Iselin, the president of
The Cooper Union. John introduced us, and Jay turned to me saying, "It's a great
pleasure to have you teaching at our school. Welcome aboard." Short of a few
experiences of being dumped by girlfriends whom I was sure loved me, I was never
so caught off guard. I tried to play it cool, thinking this was not what it appeared
to be; this was some strange academic protocol that I had yet to learn. But the
next fall, I was a visiting professor at arguably the most radical architecture school
in the world. From "zero to hero"—or professor, anyway. I was teaching a course
on my ideas titled "Sound as a Visual Medium" as part of the *Advanced Concepts
in Space* seminar series. John would come sit in occasionally but never critiqued
what or how I was teaching; he gave me free range, and I explored the notion of
sound and architecture with my students.

Among other assignments, I took the students to the Metropolitan Museum of
Art to tour the Musical Instrument Collection and then asked them to design musical instruments of their own ("form versus function" on a micro scale). In addition,
students were required to integrate their instrument into a ritual of their choice or
creation ("What act has meaning for you?").

I took them to visit different artists, composers, and architects around the city
whose work related to sound and space—performance artist Laurie Anderson,
composer Morton Subotnick, acoustician Chris Jaffe, poet Quincy Troupe, and the
film sound-editor for the Coen brothers, Skip Lievsay. I once took a class to a
Grateful Dead concert at Madison Square Garden. This was at a time when the
Dead's drummer, Mickey Hart, had just published his first book, *Drumming at the
Edge of Magic,* in which he explored the origins of drums and rituals. I got quite a
look when I presented the request for twelve tickets to the school administrator.
I was all ready to launch into my defense of it, but John walked in the office,
looked at it, and signed off with no discussion.

Once, one of my students, Frank K., was designing a "musical instrument for a
blind shaman." He was very involved in researching the way in which blind
people perceive space, and what a blind shaman's instrument might both look and
sound like. Coincidentally, that week, Ray Charles was performing at the Blue Note.
Even though he knew who Ray was, I actually had to talk Frank into coming with
us; he was reluctant to leave the design studio with so much work to do. But I
assured him this was a once-in-a-lifetime event and great "research" for his project.
Frank and I still talk about this show as one of the most memorable educational
experiences for both of us.

All of New York City is a school, and there are great opportunities for teaching in
any place and learning at any moment. I mentioned the Ray Charles incident to
Hejduk the next week. I told him how great it was to have Frank at the show, how it
was not only a first-hand experience for his research, but how our subsequent conversations gave me such a fresh perspective on teaching. John replied, "If you are
not learning from your students, then you are not teaching." This was not the first
time I thought that John knew more about what I was thinking than I did.

Question: "Mr. Charles, What is soul?"
Charles: "It's a little like electricity.
We don't really know how it works, but
it's got enough power to light a room."

maya (ma'yə) *n. Hinduism*. The transitory, manifold appearance of the sensible world, which obscures the undifferentiated spiritual reality from which it originates; the illusory appearance of the sensible world. [Sanskrit mAyA]

Christopher Janney, *Sonic Dream*.
Electronics, video, sound, dance, interactive, 1981.

Sonic Dream was an interactive instrument that tracked the movement of a dancer and triggered sound images. I designed it for myself and a dancer to communicate/interact with one another and create a single work simultaneously. It was as if the dancer were the right hand on the guitar, triggering the notes/sounds, and I was the left hand, deciding on the pitch, timbre, etc. I was working with choreographer Tom Krusinski on a version of *Sonic Dream*. I recall discussing how, if he made movements outside the environment that were similar to those inside the sound environment, it created a very interesting "sonic shadow." It was as if he were "dancing to the shadow of his own dancing."

Christopher Janney, *Soundstair Dance*.
Martha Armstrong Grey, Choreographer, 1979.

I tell students that It is easy to be complicated;
the hardest task for an artist, or anyone, is to be clear and simple.
—C. Bates

Four People in Every Conversation

1 There is "the person" in your head.
It is very clear in your mind what you want to express.
It's such a good idea, too, and all the world needs to know it.

2 There is you, the person we see, "the person" who is speaking.
True, the words are coming out of your mouth,
but are they expressing exactly what is in your mind?

3 There is the other "person" in the room hearing words from your mouth.
Does he hear all the words, or is he listening for a moment
to the birds outside and missing a key word?

4 Then there is "the person" inside his head:
processing the words he is hearing and mixing them with
his own ideas, values, thoughts.

Fifth Chakra—Blue symbolizes sensitivity, loyalty, integrity. It is the color of the throat chakra, the center of language, communication, and personal expression. When the throat chakra is in balance, we are better able to perceive and express the truth, and expressing ideas becomes easier. We are more confident speakers, and our ideas are heard more readily. Blue can help us to develop flowing, easy expression.

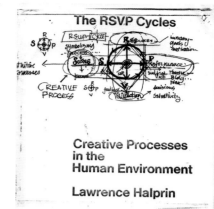

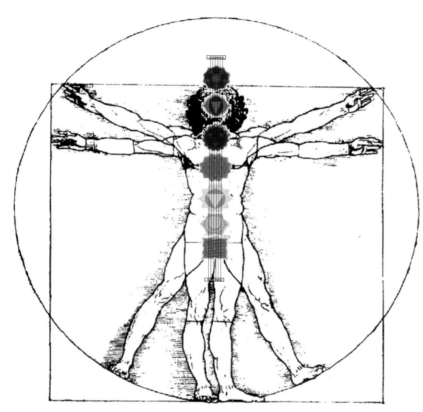

Lawrence Halprin, *The RSVP Cycles*, 1969.
Lawrence Halprin, an architect, and his wife, Anna Halprin, a choreographer, devised a unique system of notation for events that transpire over time. It was another example of expanding the idea of a musical score that could encompass more than just music. It was a system for any "temporal" art form, from dance to design, to communicate energy and intent.

The Wailing Wall, Jerusalem.
At the traditional site of the Jewish Pilgrimage, this wall, this "architecture as medium," provides the oppurtunity to try to touch the soul. Here, "the other person" is within.

Christopher Janney, *Soundstair: MetMusArt.* Sound, electronics, interactive, 1990. *Soundstair* started as my Masters thesis at MIT in 1978. From there, I built a touring version, which I took all over the US and Europe to music and art festivals until 1994. There are versions permanently installed in museums across the US, including the original one, which lives in the Boston Museum of Science.

When critiquing my own work, I like to see where it sits on this line. If it's too OBVIOUS, it's flat, boring. On the other hand, if it's so ABSURD that one can't understand it or any relationships within it, then, for me, it's in the ether. In discussions with my students, I asked for examples of each.

OBVIOUS   **ABSURD**

Kiss's *Detroit Rock City*   Damien Hirst's *Away from the Flock*
The movie *Mean Girls*   David Lynch's *Eraserhead*
Wayne Newton's *Moon River*   Def Leppard's *Pour Some Sugar on Me*
Elvis painted on velvet
Norman Rockwell's *Sunset*

Where is a good spot on the line? Right of center for me.

It's more absurd than obvious, but it's not so absurd that you can't get a handle on it. There are "hooks" into it, whether it's the reality of stairs, or waiting on a subway platform, or looking out through transparent tinted glass at the real world.

> **If you go where it's at, by the time you get there, it'll be gone. So go where it's not and keep your eyes and ears open.**
> **—C. Bates**

From the Obvious to the Absurd

But it has enough absurdity in it that it leaves questions, ignites curiosity, sparks imagination—a "musical stair" on your way to work? Waving your hand (and not saying "hi" to anyone in particular) in an impersonal environment (like an underground subway); walking through waves of colored light and approaching the childhood dream of being "inside a rainbow."

Then there is the case when the obvious and the absurd are very close together. Like in the case of some Minimalist art:

Terry Riley's *In C*, 1964
Robert Wilson's *Deafman Glance*, 1970
Carl Andre's *Equivalent VIII*, 1966
Steve Reich's *Four Organs*, 1970
Donald Judd's *Untitled*, 1969

This, to me, is what makes good Minimalist art so powerful. The good stuff is both boring and absurd but not absolutely one or the other. The counterpoint sparks a sense of imbalance, questioning, unresolved issues, curiosity, sometimes (mis)leading to thought-overload, "the less there is, the more there is to talk about."

Christopher Janney, *Reach: New York.* Sound, light, electronics, interactive, 1996. "I live on 32nd Street and am always using the subway and passing by your work. What amazes me is that people who are young and old, people who speak English and those who speak no English, people who look rich and people who look poor—they all seem to enjoy your work. This is quite amazing for a work of art. I got to thinking that you have brought more enjoyment to the world than all the politicians combined."
—From a letter addressed to the artist

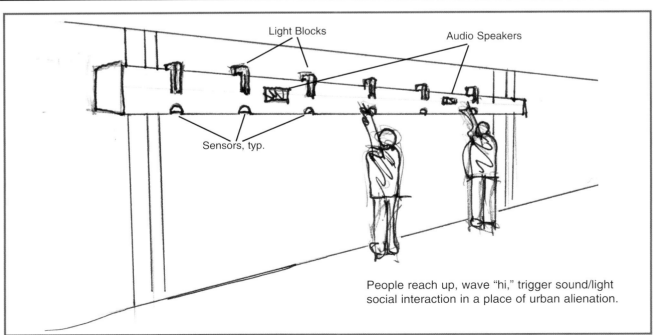

Light Blocks

Audio Speakers

Sensors, typ.

People reach up, wave "hi," trigger sound/light
social interaction in a place of urban alienation.

Someone once asked if I was to be marooned on an island with only one of my works, which would it be. Would it be *Soundstair*? Assuming I had access to electricity and all the support equipment I needed, I could play with its endless possibilities of electronic sound and sampling.

Without hesitating, I answered that it would always be *HeartBeat*, because there are elements in it that I will never be able to control. For me, it is the "dance" between the idea and its realization: the desire to control the technology in order to create new forms of expression versus creating a work, a situation, structuring an event, and letting go, riding along with everyone else to wherever it takes us.

It's a game of sorts. I make the rules, create the structure, but to complete the piece, I have to allow *nature* to come in and interact. And the closest to pure nature, to fundamental rhythm, is the human heart, with all its complexities. It is both a sophisticated pump and as the bearer of untold memories of love—first, broken, unconditional. It's still the heart and its primal sound.

Creative work is not a selfish act or bid for attention on the part of the actor. It's a gift to the world and every being in it. Don't cheat us of your contribution. Give us what you've got. —Steven Pressfield

Marooned on an Island

1. DANCER- Stand up, move over to Sax player.

2. Sax player moves out on to stage.
   Begin with improvisation over "My Funny Valentine."

Move into 3rd/flat 7th Blues.

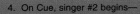

3. Dancer dances "duet" in call-and-response with Sax.

4. On Cue, singer #2 begins—

12345678	123456	1234	123	12	1111	1111	1111	1111
22345678	223456	2234	223	22				
32345678	323456	3234	323					
42345678	423456	4234	423					
52345678	523456							
62345678	623456							
72345678								
82345678								

5. Singer 1 recites text—

The upper limit of vulnerability is the stimulus above which an electrical stimulus can no longer induce ventricular fibrillation in the heart. Because ULV correlated well with the defibrillation threshold, studying the mechanism by which shock reaches ULV may have relevance to the mechanism of the heart and defibrillation. With S2 between 20 an 80 milliamps, activity could often be initiated with unidirectional conduction. This wavefront circulated around the S2 site then reentered through this site as these cells recovered their excitability. We conclude that successful defibrillation occurs because the graded responses further prolong the stimulated heart rate.

Baryshnikov/Janney/Rudner, *HeartBeat:mb.*
Sound, electronics, performance, 1999.

In August of 1999, Mikhail Baryshnikov asked Sara Rudner to choreograph a piece for him. Sarah then asked me if I wanted to work with her to set the piece I had originally created for her, *HeartBeat*, on Misha. So there I was in a studio at Lincoln Center, working with two of my favorite performers for a month—a nice slice of artistic heaven.

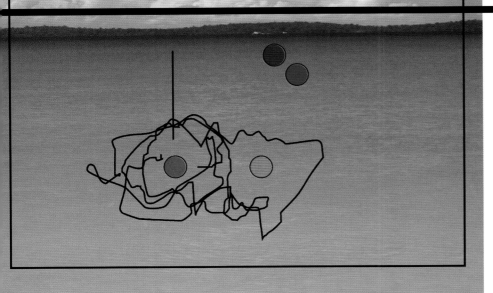

Photo Credits

106-108: Photos by David Duncan Livingston

109-111: Renderings courtesy PhenomenArts, Inc.

112-119: Photos by David Duncan Livingston

120: ©Bill Horsman Photography

121: Photo by Christopher Janney

122: ©Bill Horsman Photography (top); Plan by Christopher Janney/PhenomenArts, Inc. (bottom)

123: Plans by Christopher Janney/PhenomenArts, Inc.

124-126: ©Bill Horsman Photography

127: Plans by Christopher Janney/PhenomenArts, Inc. (left); ©Bill Horsman Photography (right)

128-131: ©Bill Horsman Photography

132: ©Bill Horsman Photography (top); Drawing by Christopher Janney/PhenomenArts, Inc. (bottom)

133: ©Bill Horsman Photography

134: Postage stamp design by Christopher Janney

135: Photos by H. Talbi

"Sonic Reflections"

138: ©Roim/Dreamstime.com (top left); Courtesy Center for Creative Photography, University of Arizona, ©Hans Namuth Estate (top right); Drawing by Christopher Janney (middle); Hulton Archive/Getty Images (bottom)

139: Duchamp, Marcel. "The Bride Stripped Bare by Her Bachelors, Even (The Large Glass)." Philadelphia Museum of Art: Bequest of Katherine S. Dreier, 1952, ©2006 Artists Rights Society (ARS), New York/ADAGP, Paris/ Succession Marcel Duchamp (top); From Lefton L, Brannon L, Psychology, 9e. Published by Allyn and Bacon, Boston, MA, ©2005 by Pearson Education, Reprinted by permission of the publisher (bottom)

140: ©Corbis (top left); ©iStockphoto.com/Mike Morley (bottom right)

141: Stewart Charles Cohen/Digital Vision/Getty Images (big); ©iStockphoto.com/Peter Chen (small)

142: Photo by Christopher Janney

143: Courtesy PhenomenArts, Inc. (top, bottom); Angelo Cavalli/Imagebank/Getty Images (middle)

144: Motown Records/Universal Music Group (top left); CBS Photo Archive/Hulton Archive/Getty Images (top right); Hans Neleman/Photonica/Getty Images (middle top); ©iStockphoto.com/David Stockman (middle bottom)

145: Photo by C. Taylor Crothers

146: Doug Menuez/Iconica/Getty Images (top); Photo by P. Franklin (bottom)

147: Capitol Records (top); Courtesy Revels, Inc., Watertown, MA (middle left); Courtesy Christopher Janney (middle right)

148: Lee Balterman/Time Life Pictures/Getty Images (top); Courtesy Simon Glynn (www.galinsky.com), ©2006 Artists Rights Society (ARS), New York/ADAGP, Paris/FLC (middle); Collection of Christopher Janney (bottom)

149: Kandinsky, Wassily. "Improvisation 31 (Sea Battle)." Ailsa Mellon Bruce Fund. Image ©2006 Board of Trustees, National Gallery of Art, Washington, ©2006 Artists Rights Society (ARS), New York/ADAGP, Paris (top); Courtesy PhenomenArts, Inc. (bottom)

150-151: ©Bill Horsman Photography (background)

150: Courtesy m/a/z/e (www.maze1971.com) (bottom)

151: ©Bill Horsman Photography (middle left); Renderings by PhenomenArts, Inc. (right); Lester Lefkowitz/Imagebank/Getty Images (bottom right)

152-153: ©Bill Horsman Photography (bottom)

152: Courtesy Merce Cunningham Dance Company, Photo by Richard Rutledge (middle)

153: Youngerman, Jack. "Black Juba." (1980), ©Jack Youngerman/ Licensed by VAGA, New York, NY (top)

154: Duchamp, Marcel. "L.H.O.O.Q." Philadelphia Museum of Art: The Louise and Walter Arensberg Collection, 1950, ©2006 Artists Rights Society (ARS), New York/ADAGP, Paris/ Succession Marcel Duchamp (top); Duchamp, Marcel. "With Hidden Noise." Philadelphia Museum of Art: The Louise and Walter Arensberg Collection, 1950, ©2006 Artists Rights Society (ARS), New York/ADAGP, Paris/ Succession Marcel Duchamp (middle); Rendering and photo courtesy PhenomenArts, Inc. (bottom left and right)

155: ©Bill Horsman Photography (top left); Photo by W. Edwards (middle right); Le Corbusier, Bruxelles: Pavillon Philips, 1958, ©FLC/ARS L1(3)47, ©2006 Artists Rights Society (ARS), New York/ADAGP, Paris/FLC (bottom)

156: Photographer unknown, Courtesy Christopher Janney

157: Photo by Kevin Noble, Courtesy The Noguchi Museum, New York, ©2006 The Isamu Noguchi Foundation and Garden Museum, New York/ Artists Rights Society (ARS), New York (left top); Courtesy PhenomenArts, Inc. (right bottom)

158: Courtesy PhenomenArts, Inc. (top, middle); ©iStockphoto.com/Florian Rieder (bottom)

159: Photos by J. Mitchell (left top and middle); Photos by PhenomenArts, Inc., ©Jack Youngerman/ Licensed by VAGA, New York, NY (middle, right); Photo by D. Lippincott (bottom)

160: Photo by Susan Schwartzenberg, ©Exploratorium (www.exploratorium.edu) (top left); Silence ©1961, Reprinted by permission of Wesleyan University Press (top middle); Cage, John. "Chess Pieces" (ca. 1944). Private collection, Chicago, Illinois, Photo by Brian Franczyk, Used by permission of Henmar Press Inc. (top right); Courtesy Merce Cunningham Dance Company, Photo by James Klosty (bottom)

161: Photo and rendering courtesy PhenomenArts, Inc. (right top and middle); ©iStockphoto.com/Buretsu (bottom)

162: Photo by Jose Pelaez, Courtesy The Irwin S. Chanin School of Architecture of The Cooper Union (top left); ©Hélène Binet (top right); Rizzoli International Publications (middle)

163: Courtesy Ritchie Israel (top, upper middle); Courtesy Yevgeniy Verbitskiy (lower middle); RDA/Getty Images (bottom)

164: Photo by D. Dubusque (left); Photo by A. Bray (right)

165: With permission from Lawrence Halprin (top right); Composition by Christopher Janney (middle); AP Photo (bottom)

167: Photo by E. Bernhardt (top); Drawing courtesy PhenomenArts, Inc. (bottom)

168-169: ©Logiman j Gamad/Dreamstime.com (background)

168: ©ILYA NAYMUSHIN/Reuters/Corbis (left); Win McNamee/Getty Images (middle); ©Karen Roach/Dreamstime.com (right)

169: Score by Christopher Janney (left); Photo courtesy PhenomenArts, Inc. (right top); Photo by Gary Friedman, With permission from the Baryshnikov Dance Foundation (right bottom)

Index

ON THIS PAGE THERE IS A DOOR
A SPIDER TO THE WEB WHERE THERE IS MORE

PAINTED WITH AN INVISIBLE HUE
USE THIS KEY TO PASS ON THROUGH

IT'S NOT SOLID, MY MATERIAL OF KIND
ENTER THE PHRASE BELOW TO GET THE NEXT SIGN

www.janney.com/_ _ _ _ _ _ _ _ _